"A desperately needed, compassionate, wise, and most of all, helpful resource for navigating the hidden dynamics of friendships. This is the book for anyone who's ever felt like a bad friend (read: everyone) or wishes they could understand why they've been dumped, ghosted, or otherwise left behind in a friendship. It's a warm hug and the nudge you need to reconsider the meaning of friendship and what it means to be a good one."

—Laura McKowen, bestselling author of *We Are The Luckiest*

"Friend breakups are heartbreaking, confusing, and often maddening. We desperately want to know how and why things fell apart. How to Be a Bad Friend *breaks down the what, why, and how of friendship in a clear and compassionate way. It shows us how our earliest relationships impact our adult friendships. And it invites us to explore deeper, more honest connections by letting go of friendship labels and unspoken expectations. In the end, it's a guide to befriending ourselves so that we can show up more fully in the world, imperfections and all."*

—Gina DeMillo Wagner, *New York Times* contributor and author of **FORCES OF NATURE: A Memoir of Family, Loss, and Finding Home**

"This book is so needed in a world that rarely acknowledges the deep heartache hidden in broken friendships. I am grateful Katherine has gifted us with her tender, honest and bold heart as she offers a way to understand and heal in some of our most intimate relationships—our friends."

—Cathy Loerzel, MA, coauthor of *Redeeming Heartache*

"How to Be a Bad Friend *is an invitation to love the wholeness of who we are, even the parts we'd like to throw out with the trash. The book is beautifully relatable, bringing us into conversation with the stories we've told ourselves about who we are to others. Katherine's writing is lyrical and comforting, like a good friend walking you through the very charged and often unexplored topic of friendships lost."*

—Sarajane Case, author of *The Honest Enneagram and The Enneagram Letters*

"From birth we are immersed in an ocean of expectations, desires, loves, wishes and fears, out of which we gradually become. As we enter adulthood, friendship becomes the fraught arena within which we grapple with, and play out, this complex interconnectedness between I and thou. In How to Be a Bad Friend *Katherine helps the reader reflect on this central dimension of our lives, with all of its frustrations, antagonisms and conflicts. With openness, honesty and grace, Katherine guides the reader into the difficult, yet profoundly rewarding work, of discovering ourselves through an uncompromising reflection on how we interact with those who mean the most—and occasionally the least—to us."*

—Peter Rollins, author of *The Divine Magician* and *Insurrection*

HOW TO

BE A

BAD

FRIEND

HOW TO BE
A BAD FRIEND

The Hidden Life of Failed Relationships

KATHERINE SLEADD

Published in the United States of America

Ash & Hill Publishing

ISBN: 979-8-218-18580-0 Paperback
ISBN: 979-8-218-18774-3 Ebook

For anyone who has lost a friend

There is so much life in you

CONTENTS

WILD GEESE

by Mary Oliver[1]

You do not have to be good.

You do not have to walk on your knees

for a hundred miles through the desert, repenting.

You only have to let the soft animal of your body

    love what it loves.

Tell me about despair, yours, and I will tell you mine.

Meanwhile the world goes on.

Meanwhile the sun and the clear pebbles of the rain

are moving across the landscapes,

over the prairies and the deep trees,

the mountains and the rivers.

Meanwhile the wild geese, high in the clean blue air,

are heading home again.

Whoever you are, no matter how lonely,

the world offers itself to your imagination,

calls to you like the wild geese, harsh and exciting —

over and over announcing your place

in the family of things.

INTRODUCTION

The first line of Mary Oliver's poem is probably the loveliest way to say what is most true about becoming ourselves. Our lives begin by being told to be good, to behave, that we have to actively work against what we would naturally become without influence. We learn this as children, or we don't, but we all grow into a world where good is wanted. Good people, good lives, good marriages, good relationships, even good money, and perhaps our most treasured one of all because of its nuance and pure indefinability: good friends. We learn to be this way, to at least try to be this way. A lot of us learn to fail, we accept the failure, we learn and grow and get back up again. We may even start to question the system of good that surrounds us, to say it doesn't matter, to grieve a loss and then find meaning. But in a way, we never really change the paradigm; in a way, we all secretly still keep trying to be just what Mary Oliver said we didn't have to, because if good is not required, what are we supposed to be? In telling our past relationship stories, we often hide what's "bad" by making it something we've "learned." We lock that bad part of us away, drowning out its voice with selfless acts, really good listening, or remembering details, holding tightly to our surviving or thriving relationships like a balloon tied to a frayed string of belief that at least there's some people we can count on. We live on, let time do its thing, and say, "It just wasn't meant to be," hoping our inner hidden world of failure will only show up every now and again as doubt or an unpleasant but respectfully mourned memory. At least, that's what we do inside our heads.

In real time, we learn to use words like *boundaries, toxic, cancel, weird vibes, block, unfollow, ghosted,* or my personal favorite, *unhealthy.* We use these words about those in our past while still in pursuit of good friends or maintaining the identity of ourselves as a good friend. We've started reading (and writing) new books and social media posts to help us understand how to be better friends, find safe people, or what being a good friend actually looks like in someone else or in us. While that might feel helpful, it's not what we need, because this pursuit of finding different or "better" or "good" when it comes to friends inadvertently deems the stories we have from our broken friendships as not good enough. This, in turn, leaves the parts and pieces of us that came alive in those friendships behind, keeping us from ever truly finding ourselves or each other. That's why we need our stories of "bad" friendships—to find the way forward to the connection we desire, bringing with us those places that came alive there, because at one point every friendship we had felt *good.*

That's what this book is about: reclaiming our bad friendship stories.

This is a book that asks, through my own stories of loss, trying to be good, and failing at even being a rebel: *Am I a bad friend?* No matter how much I wanted to or tried to get away from it, I became what I was afraid of—until I realized that being good would always stand in the way of becoming real.

Friendships, unlike any other relationship, exist because they are fluid. These non-committal connections form more of the fabric of our lives than we realize; while the majority of our relational ties might include friendship (family, colleagues, acquaintances), it's the nuance and—in a sense—polyamory of it that make friendship the connection we love. We choose each other as friends, we get to keep choosing each other, and the freedom from definition or official commitment often makes us feel as though this is something that will last forever.

Whether we build our friendships slowly or lean in fast like twin flames, we know the feeling of finding a friend in our bones. They know just what to say (or not) and when to say it. Our laughter, our tears, our gossip, our dreams, every part of us is comfortable here. It feels like the relief of taking a deep breath. And over cups of coffee, glasses of wine, a homecooked meal, or late-night snacks, we've shared our unfiltered lives. Some of us know this kind of sweetness and deep connection in unbroken cadence—sure, there've been some tough moments and hard conversations, but you made it through. And while I believe this book will offer you so much resonance and welcome, I'm writing specifically for those whose friendships met with abrupt ends: to the ghoster or ghosted, the writer or receiver of a final dramatic text, the awkward slow fade, or the silent unfollow. To lose a friend feels simultaneously like spinning out of control while trying to find a place you thought you knew. You feel worthless, used, and cast away.

We cope by leaning in to explanation and analysis where we once had a friend. We take the names and reasons of why they left and try to find answers to fill the holes in our hearts. The wounds are loud with their loneliness, and so we try to make them disappear—until the grief shows through again and a sinking feeling that there is something wrong with us, and that we might actually be the bad friend, settles in, hiding the beauty of who we truly are.

This book is a collection of bad-friend labels, ones I myself tried my very best to avoid, others that took me by surprise. Some situations may seem avoidable or weird, but that's life sometimes. I encourage you to let them be what they are to you and allow your own story to be met by these pages. I hope they give your racing mind a break and let the wounded parts in your own inner world feel less alone. It is my desire as you read that the details included or left out will allow you to sit with the hidden places of your heart. After multiple friend breakups, I felt so utterly alone—and often still do—but that is when I looked around and started noticing this is one thing we all experience but are not supposed to, and don't know how to, talk about.

A marriage ending, a romantic breakup, death in the family or estrangement—we've made room for these losses in society however we're able. We can talk about them, and our community helps us limp along toward explanation and healing for the most part. There are certainly shifts and other trials that accompany these relational events, but when it comes to friends, there is labeling or silence. Leaving us either paralyzed or having to demonize to make our way through it as we watch the ripple effect of loss extend to friends of friends, and the closing of ranks cuts deep. We don't know how to hold a relationship that never had a contract, and so we resign it to labels to make it fit with other lost connections.

In the following ten chapters, I offer a new perspective on these inner demons, an acknowledgment of their truth and their harm. As you read, may you honor and heal the wounds that you need to, may you find freedom in speaking the names you've been called out loud, along with the courage to become your beautiful complex self, and perhaps, maybe, the bad friend.

CHAPTER ONE

HOW TO BE A CLUELESS FRIEND

"I don't think the kind of friends I'd have would mind."

—Allison, *The Breakfast Club*[1]

Pre-teen years are tough on anyone. Add to that, I was homeschooled, a pastor's kid, and the oldest child—a trifecta of Type A stereotypes. Looking back, it feels like adding insult to injury that all the things homeschoolers wore then (overalls, mom jeans, denim jumpers, turtlenecks—need I go on?) are in fashion now. While I've made my peace with a hand-me-down wardrobe that was ahead of its time, I still wish I had figured out how to be a trendsetter, having dressed in thrift store clothes before it was fashionable. Seeing as I didn't attend school with my peers, my social life was scarce, but because I was a pastor's kid, youth group, for me, was sort of like middle school lite. It was my only extrovert outlet, and when I was eleven, they hosted a lip sync contest.

Continuing with the trends of being Type A, I was also a manic overachiever, and delusionally enthusiastic. For this event, I had worked out a choreographed dance (including props!) to a song by Five Iron Frenzy. They were my favorite band. They weren't actually my favorite band, but all the cool kids and youth leaders liked them, and they sang weird songs about pants and they had this song about the Midwest that was perfect for this one dance step I knew, with a line about a chicken, and I had gotten this rubber chicken that could be thrown across the stage on cue, and my hand-me-down wardrobe was already the perfect redneck costume. All I needed was a partner.

Two of my friends had already teamed up for a Steven Curtis Chapman song, which would be hard to beat, but I asked my other friend Alyssa, who said yes, to be my partner, and I promptly scheduled two practice sessions. We memorized the song in my room over two Sunday afternoons and blocked out the verse, chorus, verse, chorus, bridge in front of my mirrored closet doors. It was fun. It was quirky. We laughed a lot. I was excited—we were going to pull this off. I knew the weirder you could be, the more people would laugh. At eleven, I had already started to sense that life was not awkward if the risk of embarrassment could be on your own terms.

WHAT OUR YOUNGER SELVES KNOW

Now, as a parent of four children, one of whom is eleven, I am forced to look back on these stories so differently. In my mind's eye, that age felt big and responsible and self-aware. When really, I was still a little kid.

At the time of writing this, I am observing my five-year-old, who just started kindergarten, and basically everyone in his class whose name he can remember he considers his friend, and for those he can't, he'll ask for their name until he remembers them. At 7 a.m., rain or shine, he loudly shouts, "Hello, ___!" to everyone he sees as we walk from the car to his classroom. The risk he is taking to be friendly and enthusiastic doesn't even register for him (and it doesn't seem like risk to anyone else), and it probably won't until he one day experiences rejection.

I think that's why we love children so much because, most of all, they are present and hopeful. Our childhood friends, elementary age and younger, are for most of us, people we probably don't know anymore and wouldn't even recognize in a grocery store. Yet it doesn't even occur to us to count this as a loss because we were just present and hopeful. We might feel loss about childhood and crave moments of nostalgia from a family recipe or a walk down the street where we used to live, but there's something extra special about the way we experienced friendships when we were very young, when beginnings and endings and risks did not appear to us in the same way they do now. Even though adulthood deepens our sense of how others perceive us, as well as the sting of rejection or balm of acceptance, we still desire more in our world of what kindergarteners seem to know.

In turn, I hope we begin to create language and community that's waiting for them when they are older and friendships end in their lives. I do marvel at how, when we are young, there lives a resilient enthusiasm for connection with each other and an acceptance that some morning when we get to the next grade or change schools our paths won't cross anymore, but we will learn new names and keep saying, "Hello."

Viola Davis talks about this in her interview with Brené Brown. She talks about what belonging means for her, and she lists four things. The third item struck me:

"I apply the advice an acting coach gave me to all aspects of my life: Go further. Don't be afraid. Put it all out there. Don't leave anything on the floor."[2]

She continues on, specifically addressing how she will show up for her daughter. It's powerful how belonging and our commitment to it can look different for each of us, and yet, that commitment to being who we are to the fullest is what connects us all.

It reminds me of my five-year-old yelling "Hello!" across the school parking lot at 7 a.m., and my eleven-year-old self in hand-me-down overalls laughing with Alyssa as we threw a rubber chicken across the room.

I knew I was a lonely kid desperate for connection, but for two Sunday afternoons that summer, I wasn't alone, and I let myself delight in it. You could say my level of enthusiasm was because I was homeschooled (and you're not wrong), but it also was because my young heart somehow knew something about who I was and who I wanted to be, that silliness and lip syncing and dancing were worth the risk to take. (Where was TikTok when I needed it?) I wasn't going to "leave anything on the floor"[3] when it came to that performance, and what's more, now I had a friend with me and any perceived embarrassment would feel like more fun.

THE PHONE CALL

The day of the contest, the phone rang. My mom said the call was for me, and I picked up the landline I'd just been allowed in my room. It was Alyssa. I assumed it was about our props or costumes. It wasn't. She had called to let me know she wasn't going to do the song. I felt like the wind had been knocked out of me.

But that wasn't even the worst of it.

She continued. She told me she hadn't even wanted to come over and said her mom made her because her mom felt sorry for me. I was stunned.

As any hormonal pre-teen would, I started ugly crying. Already embarrassed on the phone call, even more embarrassed by my tears, it didn't occur to me that I could hang up. I was holding so tightly to the receiver, grasping the long, curly cord in my other hand, twisting and untwisting the loops looking for comfort. For some reason, I kept listening, and as I did, I felt a deep, new kind of embarrassment. Something I couldn't have named at the time: I felt shame.

THE WORDS BEHIND SHAME

Shame has a lot of catchphrases and names it likes to call us. In friendships, the words we most commonly hear in our heads that carry shame are some version of "I should have known better," "Why didn't I notice?" "How could I be so stupid?" or "How could I have thought we were friends?" Shame knows we do not get many chances after a miscommunication, and now with social media, even a text left on read or a post gone unliked sends us into a spiral of cataloging the last several weeks of our interactions with someone, combing through every phrase and facial expression we can remember to figure out exactly what went wrong.

On top of that, because our experiences of shame compound on each other,[4] it's scarier when we feel shame in the present to go back and remember that time when we were younger, because we've all had an Alyssa and a lip sync moment. At some point, our young and naively enthusiastic self just trusted someone at their word and thought you both were having a good time.

I hated myself for years after this, and to this day still struggle to believe someone when I say, "Hey, want to do this with me?" and they say yes, except before they can say that, I'm already hedging with "No worries" or telling them why I think what I want to do is "just an idea" and I'm "really chill either way" and "actually whatever you want to do is fine."

Translation: Just forget what I said already.

At some point, we hoped in a big way for something small and fun in connection only to be disappointed, and we swore to never again be the clueless friend.

Maybe you were one of those kids (like me) who believed someone when they said gullible wasn't in the dictionary, and even when you went to look it up, it took a minute after reading the definition to realize the joke was on you.

Of course things like that were embarrassing then, but doesn't it make you curious now? When did it become embarrassing for us to believe people? When did we learn we couldn't just say what we mean to each other?

I was a lonely, homeschooled kid, but if Alyssa had said no, I would have asked someone else, and if there was no one else, I would have dealt with the disappointment okay, although I know that's not something I can fully know. But after that day, I couldn't wrap my mind around why she would go to the trouble of rehearsals and learning and planning, wondering if she was laughing *at* me the whole time—because I had thought we both were having fun.

OUT OF THE FRYING PAN

Even before the call was over, my overly responsible eleven-year-old brain was running around behind the scenes trying to figure out what to do next. I was going to have to call and cancel my slot for the contest, or I was going to have to perform alone, or I could stay home and miss another social event in my already sheltered life. I was fine, just *fine* with being awkward, I told myself. Or so I thought, but this new embarrassment was proving to be more than I could bear. And then it got worse.

It turns out, Alyssa wasn't the only one on the phone, and when I couldn't stop crying, a voice I didn't recognize started talking to me. It was Alyssa's friend, someone I vaguely knew but not by name. She told me she was there to support Alyssa because of how I might respond. She told me it wasn't fair to Alyssa that I was upset. She told me she was sorry about how things had happened, but I was "hard to talk to" and Alyssa didn't feel like she could say no to me and Alyssa didn't like the song anyway.

Then she said something that destroyed the one thing I thought I had going for me in the world.

"It's embarrassing to be around you, and everybody at youth group knows that, and it's embarrassing for Alyssa to have to pretend to be your friend."

Alyssa's friend said all of this calmly and clearly while Alyssa said nothing. As I gulped for air in between the tears I still could not choke back, she continued on like an adult reprimanding a child, finishing with "I had to say all of this because you didn't take the hint and realize that Alyssa didn't want to say yes in the first place, that her mom made her do it."

It turns out I wasn't awkward on my own terms; apparently, I didn't even know the half of it.

Our stories often set us up for the ways we will interact later in life. For many years, I cried too easily in social situations. I wonder if Alyssa ever speaks up for herself, and I'm jealous of this unknown peer who already had the ability to articulate all these things in the face of my emotional breakdown without missing a beat.

While each one of these traits are costly in their own way, thirty-year-old me still cringes that my eleven-year-old self had a reputation for being embarrassing and too difficult to talk to about it. And that my tears proved them right.

Oof.

It was not my favorite moment. Somehow, I went to the event anyway. My youth pastor heard about what happened and, trying to be helpful, performed another song with me from the same album called "Solidarity," which would have been funny—except I didn't know what it meant (and I wasn't going to look it up in the dictionary), nor did I know the words to the song. I was supposed to pretend this collapsing mic stand was a trombone and play it for the bridge, and he had some lights set up to strobe—which was cool—but it was still three minutes of torture. I think I have more respect for what he did now than I could have acknowledged then. Alyssa was there, we didn't talk, I tried to have fun anyway and just let it go. My friends who did the Steven Curtis Chapman song won and that was that. I got home and went to bed exhausted and grateful that at least it was all over. The social event I had waited so long for had turned out to be a nightmare.

OUR YOUNGER FRIENDSHIP STORIES

We all have a friendship story like this, obviously with different circumstances and in other contexts, but essentially, we all have some moment where we let ourselves be ourselves only to find out the connection we thought was there wasn't shared by the other person.

Our social life, before we have a driver's license, is largely dependent on context (where we live, what our parents do, economic status, extracurricular activities, location of your friend's house, etc.). We're limited practically, but these things also determine some of the social rules and constructs we learn to navigate and take with us into adulthood.

Your circumstances in childhood are the context where you learn the rules of engaging with others: what is allowed, what is not allowed, what people like about you, what they do not like, what makes you a "good" friend, and what makes you "bad." For me, as a PK (pastor's kid), that meant religion and certain "Christian practices" overlayed much of my experience. While I wish what I just shared about the lip sync contest was the end of this friendship story (like I thought it was at the time), once again, it was not.

ANOTHER NEW FEELING

A few weeks later, my youth pastor called me. Apparently, Alyssa wanted to have a meeting with him, and me. I wasn't sure why, and it made me nervous. I started combing through everything I could remember about the event and the days leading up to it, and it made me feel sick. I needed another word (once again one that I didn't have at the time) for that new kind of feeling: anxiety.

We sat down in his office, and he told me Alyssa felt I hadn't forgiven her and she felt I was ignoring her and holding a grudge. I felt really lost. I thought Alyssa didn't want to be my friend, so the idea that I could still be causing a problem by not being her friend either confused me. I thought she wanted me to leave her alone, yet somehow, I was also ignoring her. I said I wasn't holding a grudge and probably apologized for the other things anyway. I did not want to have any more conversations with Alyssa; I just wanted to move on. But apparently, I was still responsible for how she felt and for making her uncomfortable—except now it was by not being around her. The embarrassment from the phone call returned, along with my newfound sense of panic.

Without any other way to process the shame and anxiety of what had happened, I boxed it up like this: I could no longer be at ease with myself or trust someone I enjoyed or believe someone enjoyed me. Being awkward on your own terms was not worth the risk, especially if you weren't paying close enough attention, and things could always get worse. There was always an angle I wasn't going to see, so I'd have to be watchful around my peers and keep my distance a little bit. Also, I guess I was responsible for other people's hidden emotions, and I'd better figure out what those were if I didn't want to get hurt.

I was a clueless friend. I had no idea people could say yes to you and mean no. But not anymore. Never again.

TURNING FRIENDS INTO LESSONS AND THE ROLES WE LEARN TO PLAY

It's easy to cast roles, and, in the telling of this story, I have. In relaying my experience of shame and anxiety, it puts Alyssa and me in oppositional parts. My reason for doing so in this, and all of the chapters to follow, is to address the idea of how we turn our failures in lost friendships, real or perceived, into lessons.

We are pattern-seeking creatures, and when something painful happens, we examine the circumstances so we do not repeat it. Just like I did at eleven with Alyssa. When we do this, we turn our real-life human interactions into scenarios, and our lost connections into ideas. Essentially, we take the story out of our bodies and into the theoretical. Sometimes that's helpful, and using the information can allow us to move forward and maybe have better relationships, or maybe not. Either way, by doing so, we have unconsciously lost a little bit of the mystery it is to love, risk, and be with one another because we've taken a multi-faceted human experience and turned it into a tidy little example.

It's the same reason why we want to know *how* someone died, *why* they got divorced, *where* the accident occurred, or *what* part of the body hurts: so we can prevent it for ourselves. Except to someone who's suffering, it's a cleverly disguised way of saying, "Everything happens for a reason" by finding out what that reason is so we can tuck it away and hope it never happens to us. Just keep your head down and stay out of it. We don't want to get close to pain we can't explain, so we diagnose, we speculate, we learn to water down the unknown, staying out of the way of harm, leaving others (and parts of ourselves) to fend for themselves.

Conversation after conversation, while researching for this book, any time I brought up the subject matter of friendship, I heard story after story from middle school. That awkward time seems to be a similar place where we all began turning friendship failures into lessons. Where we lost the freedom to just say "Hello" to a familiar face from across the room.

Do you remember those necklaces with two matching pieces, and you give one to your friend? When I was a kid, mine was a plastic heart. My daughter has one that's a magnet with a tiger holding one side of the heart. Whatever they look like, one side of the heart usually says "Best" and the other says "Friend." Did you ever give one to a friend? Did you ever receive one? Do you know which side you gave, or which side you received? Or maybe you were left out and never got one at all. Whatever the scenario, the answer is telling. Without exception, from every person I've asked, the giver kept the "Best" and the receiver got the "Friend."[5]

Friend.

In that moment, the necklace is less a token of affection, and more a role to play. The keeper of the "Best" side probably holds the main character energy, and while "Friend" is a prized title, of course, it's become a title all the same. Over the years in a relationship, or in our life, when we've boxed up all our painful experiences, being a friend can start to become a job like any other label: parent, sibling, boss, or spouse. We say friends are the family we choose, but how much choice is there in the matter? In his chapter on friendship in *The Four Loves*, C. S. Lewis says,

> But in friendship . . . we think we have chosen our peers.
> In reality a few years' difference in the dates of our births,
> a few more miles between certain houses, the choice of

one university instead of another . . . the accident of a topic being raised or not raised at a first meeting—any of these chances might have kept us apart.[6]

For as much as we love serendipity, it tells a new narrative to look at friendship this way. Obviously, we are human, and humans need connection, and our connections are largely bound by our circumstances and social context (whether we like it or not).

When our friendships change, because of new circumstances or someone else's choices, instead of seeing this as part of being human, we limit our story of connection even more through the labels we've given ourselves or each other following a breakup. We hide from our past experiences of friendship loss by condemning ourselves or our friends. We don't want to look at the places where we were rejected, the times where being our true self made us feel shame, anxiety, and so much more.

Lewis continues his thoughts on friendship by arguing that it is "the *least* natural of loves,"[7] even alluding that it is unnecessary (which sounds like something a former lonely kid would say). I would argue the opposite, that friendship is not only the *most* natural of loves but also essential to our very existence. It's the labels we give each other that are unnatural. In *Anam Cara*, John O'Donohue writes:

> The human journey is a continuous act of transfiguration. If approached in friendship, the unknown, the anonymous, the negative, and the threatening gradually yield their secret affinity with us . . . Friendship, then, is not to be reduced to an exclusive or sentimental relationship; it is a far more extensive and intensive force.[8]

Consider where you began to define what friendship meant to you and how you would describe your role as friend. It might look different for all the phases in your life, and while many of us feel the sting of betrayal or friend breakups first in middle school, you might have stories younger than this. Playmates, siblings, or lack of them, impact us as we begin to form our idea of self in the world. While we are forming our primary attachment style with our parental figures, early on, friendship weaves itself into the story of who we are and how we will connect, just as much as our parents did in our young lives. These friendship stories are telling their truth far into our futures.

Sadly, the language we have surrounding our friendships is rather utilitarian (like Lewis when he suggests they are "the least . . . necessary"[9]). We talk about friends and friendship as something to make, be, have, find, cut out, etc. Words that speak control, performance, and possession. These are the sorts of things we do not believe we actually believe, that is, until we learned our first "lesson," until we receive our first "label." Where we're no longer the five-year-old greeting everyone on our way to school, we're the eleven-year-old crying on the phone.

My first label was shame for my naivety—I was clueless, the label I constructed out of Alyssa's friend's words: "You are embarrassing to be around and don't even know it."

What stories in your friendships take you back to feelings you don't have names for? What do you tell yourself about those moments? Can you name for yourself now what you felt then? Where else do you remember those feelings from?

The deep and new embarrassment you might have easily recognized as shame, at the time I didn't. I do not believe any of us recognize it when we first learn the feeling—otherwise, it wouldn't be shame. Shame is one of those things that to name it dispels its power.[10]

If we wanted to box it up (and some days I still do), we can examine the lip sync story from various perspectives and come to those tidy conclusions: a lesson for each of us, a plan to move forward, but this would ignore the mystery of connection and the space for all the other parts of us that came alive in the friendship to be seen. To look at the story invites us to healing. To label each other locks it away.

I don't know about you, but I want to know the story.

Things we of course didn't see when we were eleven, we can see now. Things we once hid away out of shame actually offer life to us now.

One such thing I've gone back to since engaging this as a story of a friendship and not a label is the question of "Who had more courage?" The answer is we both did. The two afternoons of rehearsal were filled with play. It took risk for me to invite, to share a creative and silly idea. It took risk for her to show up when she didn't want to, and then call and speak her truth at the last minute. It took courage for us both to still go to the contest that night.

Recently I've needed to have the courage Alyssa showed on the phone that day, to say no after I had said yes, and if I'd hidden from this story and my shame, I'd actually miss out on what's available to me from this moment—and whatever else remains to be discovered in this story.

We desperately want to translate the language of harm and loss because it can feel like until we do, it will continue to haunt us. We make our grief into a why and turn whoever it was that harmed us from a human into a lesson. This can help us escape, until we find ourselves in a situation where we are in the other person's shoes. When you're finally the one making the phone call or you're the one picking up. For Alyssa to say what she meant even if she took her time, was a risk of self-acceptance in the face of someone else (me). For me to believe she enjoyed my company was a risk too. As long as we hold on to the beliefs about ourselves or others in past relationships, while that is a very normal, human thing to do, we leave behind parts of ourselves. We miss the strength of others that we discover can belong to us even through rejection—strength that someday we might actually need to lean on.

If I speculate, Alyssa probably resented herself for not saying no in the first place (which would have been difficult because her mom made her say yes), the same way I resented myself for believing her yes. Then when she finally risked it, she had to hear someone crying as hard as I was on the phone and still stick to her guns. Having a backup friend to help her with her boundary was smart because of course in that situation you're going to feel the pressure to cave.

It was a tough place for her to be, and while I know I was embarrassed for crying for a number of reasons, one being because that could imply obligation, I also wish my grief could have been accepted without it labeling me as "hard to talk to." For all we say about people's reactions, most of us would prefer them to be private, because they're often as surprising to us as they are to the other person. In any case, the friendship title was taken back.

For her to tell the truth to me, the clueless friend, meant her becoming the bad friend, the no-longer-a-friend. Then for her to say I was holding a grudge made me a bad friend. Obviously, the situation was painful for us both, and at the time, that meant one of us had to live with the blame. Blame is like that; we hand it around like a hot potato hoping it doesn't land in our lap. But it landed, first in her lap, and then in mine.

I lost some of the love of myself that day and again in the youth pastor's office, as she likely learned the cost of saying no. I became hyper-vigilant and attentive to the unspoken needs of others. I decided that everyone would be loved well by me or they would not be loved at all (which really meant I would make sure people felt liked by me even if it cost me connection with myself). She probably lost the freedom of disliking people. I would not risk my affection in friendships where I could not predict their response, and she also felt the social pressure was too cruel to risk connection. I learned to manipulate delight so I would never again be subjected to the unexpected loss of it. I learned what I could control. My mom started calling me a "social butterfly" after this, because I became *an expert* at pretending not to be lonely and having a good time. I stopped "[putting] it all out there"[11] because that meant I would be humiliated.

THE STORIES WE NEED TO REMEMBER

These are the places we need to go in ourselves and our stories when we long for more in friendship, because what we're looking for is there—it's just been locked away, because all of us are more than lessons. We do not realize we limit ourselves by however we choose to define other people. Right now, the only language most of us have for friend breakups is to take the loss of a living relationship (i.e., not death) and find a reason for it—so that we never experience that loss again, or if we do, we can ensure it will be on our own terms.

My hope is that this book will help turn us, and the friends we have loved, back from those "lessons" into humans again.

I've started here and invite you to begin where it feels safe to do so. We are all looking for belonging, within ourselves and with each other. There are many stories we hold that reveal the beauty of our unique search. Some may feel so tender and, therefore, heavily guarded. My example of middle school, a typically awkward time for us all, is a time of in-between. It reflects the discomfort and confusion in our development from child to adult, kind of like the discomfort and confusion found in the inexplicable pain of a friend breakup. Losing a friend is a form of liminal space, which is a place in us where we have lost where we once were but are not yet sure where we are going. It doesn't feel grounded, comfortable, or aligned. Yet if we bring the openness of ourselves and our curiosity to see what is there to be found, we will discover more beauty and deeper healing than if we rush through to what's defined or explainable about what has happened between us as friends.

This is the place we're invited to in friendship. It will feel a bit *clueless* as you start out, but if you decide to look backward to find your way forward, you'll begin to see parallels between your younger years and your recent past in friendship. Sometimes the things that have just happened may feel too charged (especially if you're in the middle, or just out, of a friend breakup). While our younger selves might also feel painful to explore, it can sometimes help to have a story that is not so tender to engage so we can find a way to do so with a little less judgment.

It's easier for me to hold Alyssa's perspective now than it is to offer that same compassion to friendship stories of betrayal that happened a short time ago.

It also helps to think of a friendship story where we have some sense of agency. The innocence of very young childhood may not offer as much power and choice as you need to explore such a story, and we should earn our own trust before asking ourselves to go there. With this in mind, consider engaging a friendship story somewhere between your current self and your childhood self to think about if you want to begin exploring your own friendship labels, lessons, and stories.

One of the questions we can ask ourselves as we search for a younger friendship story is: *When did we realize our enjoyment in friendship made us vulnerable?* It's a tricky place to start because *of course* friendship is a relationship where we should feel free to experience our joy. So if, after risking that, we lost a friend, we may feel like we will never have access to that freedom again. Are you aware of what happened to the vulnerability of your joy in friendship? What did you decide to believe about yourself and your friendships thereafter? What's become your role in friendships since that moment?

Until my story with Alyssa, I felt safe showing my joy with my friends. I was also blind to the nature of pity in relationships or the idea that my supposed neediness made me a target for anyone who wanted to feel better about themselves (like Alyssa's mom making her kid hang out with another kid because she felt bad for them).

From the lip sync story, I "learned" my idea of fun could be embarrassing and so I should anticipate that in my friendships, cutting myself off even more from joy. I believed how others felt about me at any moment to be something I should be able to intuit if I was to be a good friend. I also learned to find ways to pretend I wasn't hurt because that meant I was bitter. These are the "lessons" I made from the loss of that friendship.

More than anything, I learned to pay attention to all the names I was yet to be called because I was committed to never being caught off guard, trying to stay ahead of the curve to predict whether other people would label me as a friend that was good or bad. I wanted to know and expect everything that was coming at me and avoid ever feeling like I'd just picked up that curly cord landline in my room again.

CHAPTER TWO

HOW TO BE A GOOD FRIEND

"Happiness is an allegory, unhappiness a story."

—Leo Tolstoy[1]

A jeep parked in the driveway meant one thing to my six-year-old mind: the girl who was one year older than me was home, and maybe this time she would want to play. Finally allowed to cross the street by myself, I would look left, right, and left again before running over the blacktop and climbing the steps to her front door. If knocking got no answer, I would try the doorbell. Once, they let me stay for dinner and her mom made tacos. We all ate in silence, and it was the best meal I'd ever had when compared with the vegetables and plain chicken at home. They had a playset in their backyard, and this girl was cool.

I would wait at least five minutes listening intently for any sound of footsteps or voices in their house before giving up. When they finally answered the door, she would stand in the small open-ing, already taller and a step above me too, taking in my request, looking me up and down. I could always see she was deciding, and so I would wait. She never said no outright but after a year or two of "I have homework," "I have practice," "I'm busy," or "I'm tired," I finally stopped asking.

Before the lip sync contest, I was clearly not afraid of getting no for an answer. My first sibling didn't arrive until shortly before I turned seven, and I remember having to get creative as a kid to combat the loneliness of being an only child. Until then, knocking on the door at the neighbor's house across the street was the one option available to me. I naively persisted in asking day after day, willing to play whatever she wanted to play, wanting to connect with somebody my own size.

When things didn't work out, I started evaluating why, because at that age, the idea that someone wouldn't want to play with you sounded ridiculous. I wondered if I was more like her whether things would be different. She was older than me, already had two brothers, played sports, and went to a private school. Maybe those were the reasons why she didn't want to play with me, because I didn't have siblings or play sports, and went to the neighborhood school. Maybe she would be my friend if we had those things in common, but I couldn't change that. So I started wishing a family would move in next door with a girl exactly like me. My mind created a whole narrative with the conditions I thought would be necessary in order to have a "best" friend. Maybe if we were the same age, went to the same school, liked the same things, we'd have a chance at being best friends forever. When I would share about how lonely I was to my mom—she would say things like "Well, to have a friend you have to be a friend," or the old golden rule, "Treat people the way you want to be treated." I kept trying to understand what my mom meant but still couldn't figure out what I was missing, and that familiar ache of loneliness got bigger every time I looked both ways walking back across the street after hearing, once again, the answer of "no" to my tender six-year-old question of "Do you want to play with me?"

Undaunted, I continued my efforts at friendship by extending invitations to play dates, birthday parties, and imaginary games at recess. I became very determined to discover what it meant "to be a friend," but with these offers consistently rejected, I quickly learned that meant I could not expect reciprocity. I became adept at liking what other kids liked even if I didn't like it, doing what other kids wanted to do even if I didn't want to do it, to be who other kids wanted me to be even though I had no idea who I was. I didn't know then, but I was getting an early lesson in people-pleasing along with my young peers. I noticed at school that if my classmates didn't want to play what I was playing, I'd play alone. If I became too good at something and started beating others at a game too often (my only skill was tetherball), soon I'd have no one to play with. I was watching the world and saw that my level of loneliness appeared to decrease, only if my likability increased. Or so I thought.

CLIFF JUMPING AND WHO PEOPLE WANT YOU TO BE

Our parents may have asked us rhetorically, "Would you jump off a cliff if all of your friends did it?" Yet they never questioned us sacrificing ourselves if it meant we might have friends who would at least invite us to go cliff jumping in the first place. Because what parent wanted (or knew how) to deal with a socially awkward kiddo? Which meant we needed to learn "how to be a friend" to set our parents at ease just as much as we did to try to escape feeling lonely.

While there were still years of awkwardness ahead in my social life, by the time I reached my junior year, I felt I had cracked the code, even after my family moved me away from all my friends to another state. I simply built a new community again by being who other people wanted me to be. After being outed as the clueless friend with Alyssa and the lip sync contest, I took the parts of who I was that people liked and used my enthusiasm and playfulness for the things my peers (and their parents) found valuable. No one knew me, so I had the freedom of discarding the history of my "most embarrassing" stories with friendship and a way to start fresh. This time by paying closer attention to how people responded to me and allowing that to shape my desires, dreams, and behavior.

In a new town, at another youth group, I adapted to ensure my awkwardness would appeal to the desires of the popular girls as a pity project but kept my quirkiness just enough to build rapport with the quieter kids. While I never truly belonged, I wasn't alone because I became useful. I quickly changed from the socially inept girl who held tightly to what she liked and loved, and figured out how to become the woman who expertly met the needs and expectations of those around her, maintaining enough individuality to keep people entertained.

I learned how to be not just a friend, but a really good friend.

You're probably not reading this book if you're trying to figure out how to be a good friend. You're also probably not reading this book if you had a slew of childhood friends or you and your bestie from age eight are still out there taking annual road trips with each other. So, between us lonely people-pleasing kids, allow me to be the first to tell you that the whole best friend fantasy is actually the heart of the problem and why we are feeling so disheartened when it comes to our story of finding community. It's the reason you can go to a bookstore anywhere and find countless books on romantic relationships, divorce, and breakups. But there's hardly any that offer more than a chapter to address the pain of losing one's community. It's why people can barely talk about how painful friend breakups are before they're handing you a remedy that's just another version of how to be a good friend.

What is up with that?

Before we step into specific stories, we need to talk about what's happening when it comes to friendship and the reason why it's been missed in the conversation. Here's the deal. Our heartache around friendship runs so deep and feels so much more painful (as well as surprising) than a romantic breakup because it's part of a bigger issue. There's an entire way we've been told to do friendship, or how to be a "good" friend, and it's a fantasy we've got to break down, the same way we're doing for romance.

DISNEY TROPES AND OUR DESIRES

As a child, many of us were given a limited narrative of what romantic love looked like thanks to all the pre-2000s Disney Princess films. Essentially the plot, based on ancient fairytales strategically edited over the centuries by patriarchy,[2] goes like this: boy meets girl, girl is in distress/dissatisfied/trapped, boy falls in love and decides to save girl, girl then loves boy, and they live happily ever after.

The reason this storyline stuck around for so long is because it played to the things that reflected pieces of our inner world that were hungry to be seen. I know I fell for it 100 percent. Using what you already know of my story as an example, I did feel trapped (being homeschooled), I was often in distress (lots of emotions the adults around me didn't like), and I was dissatisfied (not a lot of friends). Being handed a story where all those things would be magically solved one day if only I was desirable enough to a male main character was part of the conditioning that got me through my isolated childhood, as did the promise of a BFF if only I learned how to be a good friend. While Disney fairytale messaging likely impacted us in different ways, we are starting to recognize, at least when it comes to our romantic lives, that this narrative we were fed as children only served to keep us bound to someone else and their reflection of who we are. It's backward to so much of what it means to be human, and thankfully, we are changing the ways we talk about romance now.

We're becoming free from the idea that we are supposed to be completed by another person, or that our romantic relationship or marriage has to last forever to be honored, or that we have to be married, or that love is limited by one's gender identity or sexuality. And thank goodness!

Here's the thing though, the main reason we ever got caught up in all the bullshit of those ideals and the labels of "good" and "bad" when it comes to romance is because these stories spoke to very real and beautiful desires we all have. Or at least what we're told to have if we want life to be meaningful, and what human from age eight to eighty doesn't want that?

Desires like *forever*—something natural to want yet impossible to have for a human who knows death is the one thing that's certain—were boxed up and marketed to us as "Prince Charming" and lifelong marriage with "the one." Other desires too, like peace and belonging, things that are hard to find in a world (or perhaps one's own family) filled with chaos and discord, were handed to us through TV shows that resolved every conflict or preached at us from a pulpit telling us what "good" is. For whatever we wanted, there was a story we were told about what it truly was we desired, how to want it, where to get it, and that as long as we were good enough, it would work out. This essentially says, *Here is what is not allowed and here is what is accepted, and if you step outside these lines, any disruption is your fault and not something wrong with what's going on around you.* Thus, many of us learned (or at least tried) to be good by avoiding conflict at the expense of our boundaries and seeing others really well while making ourselves invisible.

Think for a moment, what else were you taught to change about yourself in the hopes of receiving something you longed for? Can you see how very real and deeply human the cores of these desires are, and that some of them are still within you? Of course, we want the goodness of loyal connections, someone we can find rest with and reflection: friendship's version of happily ever after, which is essentially "we're not alone, we'll never be alone, and everything is going to be just fine as long as we find the right person."

Since then, we've done a better job of unpacking how messed up the romance narrative is, and we're starting to see the freedom that brings for our relationships. We're starting to realize forever could be experienced through a lifetime of different loves, or that true peace actually requires conflict. We're discovering more of the truth Mary Oliver evokes in "Wild Geese," liberating us from relationship standards around who and how we love—at least when it comes to our dating life.

Returning to the truth of our desires and deconstructing the happily-ever-after trope has changed the way we approach the expectations of romance, bringing more curiosity for what we, individually, might want in connection with each other. We are happier leaving society's antiquated standards behind, but we need to realize that we still have some of the desires that sold us on the Disney film in the first place. The only difference is, we've decided those things are not worth expecting from romance. Instead of collectively owning the desires that got us caught up in the fairytale, we pretend we never needed or wanted them in the first place. Except that wasn't entirely true, we just handed the job of maintaining those standards off to a different type of relationship. And yes, you guessed it, that would be our friendships.

There's a lot of reasons we try to escape desires, especially ones that have gotten us into trouble, because our desires make us vulnerable. Just like how my desire for connection as a kid won out lots of times over something I wanted to do, or cost me through rejection. Much of life is learning to live in the tension of that, between what we have and what we want,[3] and what's important as we continue this journey of healing your friendship story and stepping closer to the pain of the labels and expectations you've lived under, is that you know *there's more at play* when it comes to that friend breakup you feel ashamed of.

THE FANTASTICAL FRIENDSHIP FAIRYTALE SOLUTION

What we've been taught is this: we have a "problem" that is either our loneliness or parts of ourselves we've been conditioned to hide and are afraid will cause rejection if they are seen. Then, because we live with that fantastical narrative for friendship, the solution is a "good" or "better" friendship. We want someone to give us the feeling we found with a BFF in childhood that we secretly hope results in a lifelong commitment to each other to "ride or die," friendship's version of "for better or for worse." We long for anything that resembles the innocence of childhood connection and our inner eight-year-old is still making plans to be bonded for life.

We still have a friendship version of happily ever after, all that it relies on is for us to be a good friend. Have the right boundaries, hold space in the best way, know how to apologize well, set aside enough time, keep showing up . . . phew! Are you exhausted yet? Or maybe a better question is: Does it make a little more sense now why being or having a good friend and this whole "find your people" thing feels less like living in reality and more like the weariness of trying to have a romantic relationship that looks like the plot of an old Disney princess film?

While we can look back on early childhood stories of friendship and think, *Oh, how sweet*, the ache there is more like nostalgia than the constant pain of loneliness that just won't go away. As adults we're trying to navigate a world where one of the bestselling books on friendship is *still* Dale Carnegie's *How to Win Friends and Influence People*. It's a book mainly based on manipulation and sales tactics—but you better believe the people around you will think you are a very good friend if you start applying them. Which will work just fine until you burn out and realize you're just as lonely as ever.

The truth is, as adults we're living in a world where we know that if we have a conflict with one person that can't get resolved quickly, there's a good chance of being ghosted or, worse, gossiped about with the ultimate catastrophic result of losing our entire community depending on who else believes the rumor mill. Our social life is perilous, and we've been handed a fantasy that some-where out there is a group of friends that will be with us no matter what. You just have to "find your people." Are you starting to see it now? How the whole quest to find your bestie is not that different from the search for "Mr. Right"?

We have a friendship problem, but relying on a fairytale of how to be a good friend that will fix it is part of what's keeping us stuck. We're scared of the alternative—if we're not already living in it—which is a total loss of community and the feeling that we are unwanted by anyone who even glimpses the truth of who we are.

I know. I've been there, twice actually, but not for the reasons you'd think. I didn't really lose my community because I did some-thing "wrong" but because I stopped being the good friend—the friend I'd learned how to be in order to have friends.

FINDING LANGUAGE FOR LOSS

The weight of our own loneliness and the weight of society's un-spoken demands of friendship, and more, is just a glimpse as to why friend breakups hurt so damn much. On top of that, the reason it feels impossible to talk about or figure out is because we don't even have language for it yet. And when we don't have language for something, that's often a sign of trauma.[4] A friend breakup is a form of trauma. Calling it trauma might feel startling, or over-the-top, which is fair. Who's met a person who enjoys having something called trauma be a part of their life story? We count ourselves "lucky" to avoid it. The truth is, for all the "big" events, or catastrophes, or what we read in survivors' stories that are trauma, there are so many smaller and more subtle things that are trauma too.[5] It's important to name (meaning, to call something what it is) the smaller things too; otherwise we won't be able to access the healing we hope for to ease the pain we are feeling, much less reclaim the parts of ourselves we had to hide away, even if the trauma that happened was a fallout with a friend.

As it stands, without acknowledging our hidden desires or addressing it as trauma, the only tools we're applying to deal with moving on from friend breakups are some pretty restrictive labels. The popular ones that come to mind are *toxic, dramatic, unhealthy*—each of which we will unpack in later chapters, that uniquely speak to desires in us that went unseen, as well as traumas that have gone unnamed. We generally agree on these definitions as a society, making it easier to explain away in a conversation with someone why you're no longer speaking to your friend anymore. But this kind of simplification misses the entire world your friendship was and what needs to be cared for and healed in order for you to feel truly free in connection with someone new again.

Of course we're all desperate for a solution—like a step-by-step handbook on how to be a good friend. But that will never give us the answers we long for, just like the classic villain trope in every fairytale isn't telling the whole story. Our labels for each other have so much more to say about what we need and what happened than we are willing to give them credit for, but when we don't know how to talk about something or, more accurately put, we don't feel safe to talk about it, what do we do? While we do need to be brave and try to figure out how to talk about that thing, more importantly we need to ask *why*.

Why haven't friendships and friend breakups been something we talk about?

Before I make this too complicated by getting into the societal structures that keep us divided, let me ask you to imagine a world where we could break up with our friends, or they us, and we could talk about it freely in order to heal in shared community spaces without shame.

It's hard to picture, isn't it? Because that would change almost everything—illuminating that perhaps our issue with friendship is less the loss of the friend but rather that we do not feel we can speak about it.

When we start to look at why friend breakups have not been talked about, we realize this problem is about more than just "creating" language for something we don't have language for.

A culture where individuals can have and metabolize conflict, and hold space for the complexity of all that is friendship, is a culture that can affect change at a broader level because it's a community that is no longer built on shame. Which is not the world we live in. Colonial and patriarchal structures are largely responsible for this.[6]

NORMAL PEOPLE, BAD BLOOD

Let's use reality TV as a simple example. Many of these shows' premises are built on the tension generated by "toxic" relationships between women. We rarely, if ever, see friendships portrayed in any real sense where bad blood between two people gets to be perceived as normal, or as part of how flawed human beings relate to each other. Because when you allow people to have conflict without shame, eventually they learn how to work together.

Take any of the beloved comedies we know and love as a culture and notice how the friends are friends through all the seasons, and if they hit a rough patch, they find a way to work it out. If someone does leave the show, we know it's only because they got written off or took a new job. Even in our stories of friendship, we construct a "perfect" world where the reliability of forever, and the resilience needed to get there, is woven into every episode. No wonder we feel like failures when it comes to lost friendship or loneliness when even the quirkiest characters find a place to belong.

The trouble is, the construct we're being handed of the good friend as a way to create a new paradigm, is part of that same system. We're still looking for other people to fulfill a list of qualities even we couldn't live up to (a.k.a. Prince Charming) and simultaneously wonder why we feel like shit for being human (we are not Snow White just "whistling" while we clean up other people's messes). Worse yet, we're burnt out because we can't keep up the act of being a good friend with any room for our lives to fall apart.

So what do we do with this longing for good friendship that carries the hidden hope of forever along with other desires?

First, we acknowledge that some part of us wants it (or has been told to want it—both or either can be true).

Second, we look around us and get honest with ourselves that while we might be fine with or without forever, we aren't sure how to get out of the old narrative. Because no one's shown us how.

Part of the way forward involves naming what we desire from friendship, and the way we want to be able to show up in friendship. This might feel obvious, but it is easier said than done because we are also unraveling what we were told to want and who we were told to be in order to have connection. Discovering which parts of us bought into those requirements is important because it reveals where we've had to distance ourselves from our own desires while also paving the way for us to find them again.

HOPE FOR A NEW NARRATIVE

While Disney films and patriarchy created the narratives that have kept us bound up with desires that aren't ours (or we want to pretend aren't ours), in order to get out, we need to talk about the impact of another type of story. Every friendship we have ever had is its own story, along with all the little moments that led us there, that we shared, or that meant it ended. Stories shape so much of who we are, both the ones we read, and the ones we tell ourselves.[7] Some stories *tell* us what we should want, others *reveal* what we most deeply long for. These are the stories we revisit again and again because they remind us of our desires and the way we want life to be and feel. J. R. R. Tolkien's classic fantasy series is one of these stories for me.

I had a phase (but let's be honest, it's not a phase) where I was obsessed with *The Lord of the Rings*. I did a book report on it dressed up as Legolas in the second grade. (They hadn't even started making the movies yet.) I loved those books, and years later could quote the film as if it was a sing-along because I watched them every Friday night through high school without fail as the sequestered homeschooled child I was.

The Lord of the Rings is an epic story, and I don't know if you've ever noticed, but friendship is the start of it all. For those of you who don't know this story, just stop everything and watch all three movies and then come back. I'll wait. Okay, I realize that's unreasonable and it's fine if you don't, so here's an overview (spoiler alert).

In the world of Middle Earth, there are a number of beings: elves, dwarves, men, orcs, hobbits, and a few wizards. As the story goes, a ring of power created by a dark lord falls into the hands of the smallest of creatures, a hobbit. At first, he doesn't know what it is and the ring gets tucked away until it's passed on to another hobbit who is good friends with a wizard. It takes time for them to discover just what is in their possession.

Once they realize the ring is a source of power, and then realize in the hands of any living creature such power would only bring destruction, a group is brought together. They're all different, some of them friends, several sworn enemies. But with a common purpose for the good of Middle Earth, they agree to journey together to save everyone by destroying the ring. Though no promise binds them together to do so.[8]

Needless to say, things get complicated and tense as any of us would if we went on a long-term backpacking trip with the fate of the world resting on our shoulders. Friendships are strained and objectives clash, surrounding danger unites them for survival, and moments of rest simply allow the distrust and conflict to grow. Eventually, "the fellowship" is broken.

It's an epic tale that invites you to a world that is not your own, to witness a community fighting for the collective good while wrestling with demons of their own, persevering through interpersonal tension. No one is waiting on somebody else to show up, and each character with their doubts and flaws brings their authentic selves—not knowing if it's going to save the day.

WHAT WE REALLY WANT

Those stories are the kind of stories that give us access to language we can't, or won't, verbalize about our lives and desires. They help us process what we really want, find the things we hope for, grieve what we've lost, and embody truth in a way "deep conversations" might never compare with. They're often disruptive in exactly the ways we won't allow ourselves to be, or acknowledge our inner worlds are.

Whenever someone says they don't like conflict, a part of me wants to poke them by asking if they enjoy movies, novels, or TV shows of any kind. Stories are built entirely on conflict, a problem that leads to a climax that may or may not offer resolution, and we love them either way. We would not pick up a novel if it did not hold an element of some form of tension, drama, or a "bad" guy.

This brings me back to how we've excluded friendship from the freedom we allow our romantic relationships from the happily-ever-after trope. While we need to be liberated from the arbitrary rules put in place largely by society, we aren't acknowledging the desires we had underneath the surface those structures played to in order to get our buy-in to a certain narrative.

Part of us still wants forever, and the conflict and drama that goes with the struggle to reach it. We might think we don't, but we actually do. It comes out in the ways we choose to escape our reality and in the way we characterize those who are connected to our reality, namely our friends. Instead of acknowledging that, we end up isolating and othering when someone doesn't show up to our hidden desire for some version of happily ever after, when the truth is, we know our longings are so much bigger than the limitations of just being a good friend or a happily-ever-after kind

40

of story. But it's scary to own that and move into a narrative that's larger than what we've been told to want.

It's difficult to see because as all our forms of romantic relationships move toward greater freedom and acceptance in our culture, we don't realize our desire for some of those "old narrative" components remain. Yet every story that's ever captured us in that front row seat spectacle *has* played to our desires. We might easily identify what is wrong with the narrative but remain distant from the things within ourselves that were captured by it.

So how do we get out?

The answer is the same as what got us stuck in the first place: stories. Your stories, to be exact. And guess what—if you've been through a friend breakup, you already have one. This is ultimately what I'm inviting you to see as you read about mine in the following pages, because stories can hold what we do not allow, or wish, ourselves to be. Finding a kind, reflective gaze that moves outside the limitations of labels you've either received from or given your friends is going to show you a world you didn't know was there. And that's where we're invited to play.

We all know how to be a good friend—that's the problem. What we don't know is how to read the stories of our real-life failed friendships with tenderness and honor, not as some "don't repeat the mistakes of the past" mantra, but as the fabric of our lives. To be with our own heartache with the same eagerness and delight as the novel we return to again and again.

Any invitation to look forward toward new or more resilient friendships must be rooted in a kind gaze toward our past. Can you read the loss that lives in your loneliness? Do you know the source of the grief and desire within your own friendship story?

When we say we want good friends, what we really mean by that is a good story. And stories, as we know, all come to an end even if they are lifelong. But so many are not, which does not make it any less of a good story. The thing is, in order to experience life and joy together, what we are really asking of ourselves and each other is a narrative that will capture our hearts and minds and bodies and transcend time in our connection with one another, however long it lasts.

It's vulnerable to step into this, and it is good, though not because we have to be but because we become present to our friendships as they were, as they are, and as we are becoming.

So let's change the narrative for our friendships with better stories.

And you know one thing that makes for a damn good story? Drama.

CHAPTER THREE

HOW TO BE A DRAMATIC FRIEND

*"Do I like being involved in Drama? No. Do I like knowing
every detail of what's going on from every single party
involved in Drama? Yes."*

—@isabelletinati[1]

*"Here is your life. You might never have been, but you are because the
party wouldn't have been complete without you. Here is the world.
Beautiful and terrible things will happen. Don't be afraid."*

—Frederick Buechner, *Wishful Thinking*[2]

If you had to make a timeline of the labels we apply to friendship,
from when we know things are going downhill to when the breakup happens, *dramatic* would be the start until you finally made it
to *toxic*.

And if letting go of being the good friend is about freeing
ourselves from someone else's impression of who we should be,
becoming the dramatic friend is about discovering the ways we
project what we are afraid of in ourselves onto our friends in order

to stay good. Drama is the first stop on our journey to being the "bad" friend.

I doubt there are many women (or humans, for that matter) who have shown honest emotion about some situation they are in, who haven't been labeled dramatic. There are even T-shirts made for little girls that say "Drama Queen" as if the developing limbic system of a small child is something to be mocked. We love drama in all the stories we pay money to read and watch, but when it gets too close to our personal lives or friendships, we don't know how to handle it.

Dramatic is a title of othering, solidifying the person given the label as the one on the stage, and the one bestowing it as a member of an audience (whether they have admitted that or not). If you're someone who finds yourself in a front row seat, you could say that a dramatic friend is essentially the toxic friend you still want to hang out with—like the TikTok quote above.

The truth is, to be alive is to be dramatic. Being dramatic means someone who feels into both the highs and lows of their life and is not afraid to be seen in that. A dramatic person is willing to take Viola Davis's advice and "put it all out there."[3] While there are people who manipulate others by how they express themselves, instead of seeing the difference between someone who is willing to be authentic and feeling and someone who is leveraging their emotions to change who you are, we lump the two together. A quick Google search will show you how common this title is in our culture, defining it as a person who is "overly" emotional.

When you hold that up to the reality that most of us come from a generation where none of us were given the tools or validation of the fact that we *have* feelings, the absurdity starts to show because the titles like "Drama Queens" and "Toxic Masculinity" go hand in hand. Women get accused of over-feeling while men shut down their feelings. This is the mess where the awareness of the dramatic landscape awakens new life inside us, which is exactly what we need to be part of changing this narrative in our world, starting with our friendships.

First, we need to expose the setup of the dramatic friend.

Here's how it works.

We're social creatures, we want to connect, and we love friendship. A close friendship is likely one of the most emotionally intimate relationships we'll have. There are things we feel free to talk about with our friends that we don't with romantic partners or maybe even our therapist, things we obviously won't share with coworkers or the cashier at the grocery store. A friendship is a place where we can be honest about our thoughts and emotional world, in a way where we are resonated with yet challenged. It's a place we feel safe enough to tell the truth and receive another perspective. These are the types of rich, fulfilling, "deep" conversations everyone's wanting when they say, "I don't do small talk."

One of the reasons we long for this is because life is difficult; it is "beautiful and terrible,"[4] and we aren't meant to hold either one of those things alone. By cultivating a relationship where we can share our unfiltered selves without fear of rejection or shame, it feels like we're creating a security deposit in case one, or both, of our worlds falls apart. Surely if we can connect on our real thoughts and someone can reflect our feelings back to us (and vice versa!) we've found that ride-or-die person, and now we're set for whatever life throws our way.

That's a brief overview of what's sometimes under the surface in our search for a good friend. We're looking for someone who is alive to life, and we want to be with them, and they us.

Here's where the dramatic label walks on stage and things get tricky.

What's fascinating about this particular label is while we are looking for and finding that "spark" of friendship and connection, we're also bringing our hidden desire for others to be there for us when our lives fall apart (kind of like an insurance policy). But so often when we, or our friends, are the ones going through a crisis, people start to look for an exit, and then we lose our friend at the moment we need them the most. Essentially when the drama word starts getting thrown around is the same moment where we would hope our people would show up for us but instead ends up being when they make the choice to walk away.

It's important to say this doesn't mean we can't walk away, or if we are, we're abandoning someone. But, just like the happily-ever-after concept and how that's impacted our friendships, we need to take a closer look at this phenomenon along with the label of *dramatic*, because it changes the way we see and are seen by our friends as individuals.

Drama surrounding friendship is a peculiar blind spot. As stated before, *dramatic* is a title of othering. To other is to distance ourselves from someone in order to protect an identity we've constructed about who we are in connection to who someone else is or isn't. We only need to other people when there is something within us that another's personality or humanness disrupts. Othering is not related to boundaries, it's when we need to preserve a fragile part of our ego by saying, "Look at me, see how I'm not like them."

We other when someone shows us a side of ourselves we pretend doesn't exist, and in the othering of calling something drama, we are unconsciously acknowledging our own participation. Similar to the question, *if a tree falls in a forest and no one is around, does it make a sound?* if a friend is going through a crisis and no one labels them dramatic, is there really a problem with how they're handling their situation or asking for help?

Given that to be alive and human is to be part of the drama that is life, most of us know the weight of these words—either from being placed on us or letting them land on somebody we once felt close to.

So, where did we learn to play these roles instead of being free to be who we are with each other?

WHERE WE LEARNED WHAT ROLES TO PLAY

Before we ever learn what society says our friendships should be, we are already in the audience seat watching our parents' connections (or other adults' lives) play out. The way they think about the world, themselves, and other people shapes the beliefs we have about someday finding love and belonging. What they told us or what we overheard, in addition to societal norms, also influences our friendships in adulthood. They shape the way we see our own life unfold, in both the beauty and terror.

It's no secret that, before we can drive, our social life revolves solely around our caregiver's availability and willingness to go out of their way to make sure we have the connection we need to grow and develop. If you were in public school, that was some degree of being with your peers but not the same as getting to just be yourself with the people you wanted to connect to.

My wishful childhood thinking of the last chapter, where I imagined the circumstances needed for a BFF, was deeply influenced by a friendship my mother had and the meaning she put on it. My mom and her friend were pregnant with their first babies (me and my friend!) at the same time, with due dates only weeks apart, which is how they connected. We ended up being born less than a month apart, and to me, that was close enough to be magical. We had basically been friends before we were even born, and growing up, we always went to each other's birthday parties. This constant along with an *almost* shared birthday made me feel like if anyone in my childhood was going to be my best friend, it would be her. Looking back, I don't know that I was her best friend, but we genuinely enjoyed each other's company and she was someone I could be myself around.

Once, in an awkward middle school moment, we found out we had a crush on the same boy (despite us both being homeschooled and having no overlap in our social life). We weren't allowed to date anyway, but she immediately responded by saying, "No, you can have him." I knew he had no idea who I was and pushed back with the same response more out of insecurity than anything else, yet I felt so startled by her valuing of our friendship that my teenage angst about this boy no longer mattered anymore. She was cooler than me in every way possible that matters at that age: her hair, clothes, social skills. She was athletic, popular, adventurous, but she didn't leverage those things over others like so many girls are conditioned to do to maintain popularity.

We stayed connected off and on through the years with not a lot of contact until my parents decided to pull me out of public school in fourth grade. I remember my friends from third grade calling my house to see which class I was in for the next year, and me telling them I wouldn't be there, saying goodbye to one after the other over the phone in the kitchen. I never saw any of them again. I didn't know how to be with the grief of what was happening and told myself it wasn't sad. My friends sounded sad, even worried for me, asking who I would get to see if I was home all the time.

I maintained that I was excited because we were going to have monthly field trips with my best friend and her family, instead of just seeing each other around our birthdays, so of course I couldn't wait. She had more siblings, and because my only sibling was almost seven years younger than I was, it always felt like a party to be with them. They had a giant backyard and our moms got along, which meant we could play for hours after whenever one of them said, "It's time to go!" because we all knew they would keep talking and eventually order pizza and it would be long past our bedtime before we finally drove home.

Up to this moment, my mom was friends with my friend's mom in a way she looked up to and enjoyed. This woman was open, kind, and helpful. When my mom became interested in homeschooling me, my friend's mom demystified the whole process for her and made it simple. This was a lot of work and to help someone learn how to do it well is equivalent to a part-time job. She taught my mom how to navigate the state's requirements, find curriculum, find community, and feel confident learning a new skill over the course of that whole school year. Walking alongside someone with that level of detail in learning a new process is a generous thing to do by any standard.

The current loneliness epidemic is showcased by how much of what we pay for is to replicate what is shared freely when we have supportive friends. I'm not advocating for life in a commune, and I believe our skills should be something we are compensated for, but the fact remains that connection is commodified in our economy. There are probably influencer homeschool moms out there charging at least five grand for what my friend's mom did simply because she cared about my mom and wanted her to succeed and knew how to help.

Something like this level of radical generosity tells us early on what's possible, perhaps expected, or even at stake, in our friendships. We take in this data less from the stories we read, and more from watching our parents navigate their social life. Their sense of satisfaction and level of trust in community influences our hope as adults of finding a place to belong. I know my desire to help my friends if I have a skill they want to learn is connected to watching my friend's mom help my mom and experiencing the goodness of being with my friend's family, and I wonder how things would have unfolded had a life-altering tragedy not occurred in their family later that same year when my mom started homeschooling me.

WHEN TRAGEDY STRIKES

You might feel that the closeness our moms felt and the exchange of help would translate to acceptance and support in their time of need (like the insurance policy we feel about having friends for when our lives fall apart). In some ways it did. If you know how to do something your friend doesn't and you share your knowledge, walking them through the scary parts of learning how to do it on their own, that's a life-changing connection. Plus, now you and your friend have a shared space where you're growing together. What's not to love? This is what my best friend's mom did for my mom, which would deepen and enrich any friendship, right?

My family did show up for them, along with others. We were over at their house nearly every day, and at ten I remember feeling confused about how happy I was to see my friend but also sad and with no idea of how to be there for her. I didn't know what grief meant, except that you made dinner for people, you listened, and you distracted them. Or did you? Were you supposed to make them laugh or help them feel safe to cry? Mostly us kids tried to keep out of the way of the adults who were always talking, and that meant we left the house one day while it was raining. We snuck onto a golf course nearby that was wildly muddy and ran around barefoot yelling and screaming without caring that we were trespassing on private property. Hours later, we came back to adults frantically looking for us, only for them to find us carrying my friend because climbing up the steep slippery hill on the way home, she sprained her ankle.

In retrospect I can't imagine how discouraged, terrified, and frustrated our moms must have been—a crisis (albeit a small one) on top of a crisis. They had no idea where we all were, and now their daughter was injured. I felt ashamed for not keeping my friend safe (which wasn't really my job, but it felt like I failed somehow).

We were children trying to understand what had happened and resisting the horror of it in the only way we knew how. Running off without telling anyone in the rain to a place we shouldn't be felt right, alive, risky, but free for maybe a brief moment in the middle of unspeakable pain. A drama that is less severe within a drama serves to give us a sense of something we can control. At least the group of us girls were on the made-up stage of that golf course screaming and laughing together in that moment while back at the house, the adults in the weeks and years following managed their experience differently.

My mom loved my best friend's mom, and she dropped everything in her life to be with her for whatever she needed both that day and for a long time after, but their friendship changed. The rift between them was invisible and, to my awareness, never acknowledged in their relationship. It couldn't be, but this tragedy accentuated it as any trauma does, highlighting the cracks that became fault lines. Part of the reason my mom knew how to show up well was because she had some experience that resonated (though not the same), and she knew what she had needed in her own grief and found a way to translate that with what she offered her friend.

The trouble was (although it's actually a very normal human thing in most relationships) she also wanted a lot of things in her life that my friend's mom had: she was a homeschooling pro, had more kids, more money, a bigger house. Can you feel how squirmy you start to get as I list those things off, especially in the context of this tragic event? My mom's friend was generous, chill, and like any human, had her own flaws—but in my recollection, she was way more relaxed than my mom, and I loved being at her house. My mom did too, but after she learned how to homeschool, and this trauma occurred, things started to change.

When the initial wave of grief slowed, and the long slow road to making peace with something that would never make sense had begun, my mom changed the way she responded to her friend and how her life was unfolding. She would say things, almost casually in passing to me in the car on the way home from a field trip, or while I would help her with dinner, about her friend. They were subtle, but the comments highlighted different aspects of her friend's life and what that meant about their family in comparison with ours. As the years went by and their whole world continued to change as anyone's does after such a loss, my mom started to attribute the pain her friend was feeling to those life changes as the result of certain "choices" her friend made, choices that conveniently were the opposite of what our family did—things as benign as their schedule, how often they had dinner together, or even a curriculum they chose to use that we didn't. To escape the pain her friend was figuring out her way through as best she could, my mom began comparing and contrasting her life with her friend's life and soon my friend's with mine.

As a child, I was puzzled but felt like I had to agree with her although I wasn't even sure how or what that meant. I didn't feel "better" than my friend, and I was so sad for what their whole family was going through and wanted to help. Now, it's clear to me that my mom wasn't able to acknowledge how her friend's pain triggered her own trauma and she needed a way to feel safe around her friend. This looked like envy masked as criticism and expressed as concern.

THE VISIBLE FORM OF ENVY

We like to think we are understanding and empathetic, but the truth is someone else's pain will inevitably highlight our own. This is where we become the critic in the audience[5] instead of staying with our friend on the stage. We turn our friend's complex life circumstances and emotionally vulnerable experience into a side-show that allows us to escape the lack of courage we have to feel our own pain.

It's a peculiar form of envy because at first glance it looks like empathy, but it's not. It's pity, which is the visible form of envy. Pity is the envy of someone's ability to be authentic and vulnerable while showing up to the pain of their experience. It is the desire to believe that if we were in someone else's shoes, we would be able to survive whatever it is they are going through. When someone shows up to the plot twist in their life with their whole self, the rage, the confusion, the uncertainty, and the chaos, we turn to pity because it's the only way to keep ourselves safe from what we fear of discovering about who we are in our own heart-ache, and as long as what's happening to someone else is dramatic, we continue to hide from who we are. We turn to pity when we envy the strength someone has to feel, without shame, the pain of their human experience in a place we hope we never have to face because it would mean a greater reckoning with ourselves to survive there.

I watched the devastating tragedy that happened in my friend's family and how the grief gutted them just like it would anyone; with shrapnel from it scattering in all areas of their life. I felt how slowly, but surely, our connection to them started to change. Things were falling apart in the quietest of ways, as was my unshakable trust in the hope of a "best friend" connection. Every time I would overhear my mother play the role of confidant when she was with her friend and switch to an observer when she wasn't, I would wonder, *Is this what my friends will do if my life falls apart?* While this wasn't a question I could have articulated at that age, I know it rooted itself in me as an uncertainty that should I ever feel unspeakable grief, I would be comforted to my face only to be criticized behind my back.

It is interesting to consider why, along with calling little girls dramatic, we say things like "oh, teenage girls are so mean," pretending we don't know how they become that way. We learned to tell our friends that we are saying what we mean and showing up authentically when we're not. This is the half-truth born from every one of us having watched the adults in our world speak out of two sides of their mouth—even about people they said they cared about the most. They told us not to lie but let us listen through the wall to learn how. This incongruence of how our parents showed up with their friends, versus what we heard when they got home, influenced us more about who we could trust or believe than playground politics ever could.

I wanted so badly to be a good friend to my friend in this terrible moment, and the confusion of my mother criticizing her friend, someone she had looked up to and who had gone through so much, was too much for my heart to make sense of. So I tucked away the belief that I needed to protect myself from being dramatic or being seen in any way that could be perceived so. And if I couldn't do either, then I would need to be prepared for the consequences should the circumstances of my life mean I took center stage.

Eventually we moved away and the connection between me and my friend dwindled, but the experience wove its way into me about how friends treat each other when things start to go wrong even when you've given them everything.

A THOUSAND LITTLE WAYS

These are the stories that play behind the scenes when we are trying to figure out friendship. The dynamics of your family and childhood are different from mine, but there are a thousand little ways we were watching and being told about how belonging works in this world. They sneak into our relationships in the present much more subtly than five ten-year-old girls climbing through a hole in the fence onto a private golf course, but they disrupt things just the same if we aren't aware of what role the adults directed us to play.

Essentially when "other" people go through trauma, there's someone backing away from the "drama," forming their own opinion of how and why "you're doing it wrong." Or even worse, if they deserve to be there.

One of the biggest things this does is solidify which character we will play in our friendships: if we're someone whose job it is to be on the stage, or if we always have tickets to the show. When the word *dramatic* comes up, it impacts us differently depending on which position we're most afraid we're in and, therefore, are afraid to acknowledge. Often this is because we are seeing a reflection of either our flaws or our goodness in what our friend is revealing about themselves.

We want to pretend we don't want what we want or that we aren't the messy humans we are, and so we find a place to sit down with a bowl of popcorn and watch someone else live the story we're afraid to engage ourselves. We choose friends who are "better" and "worse" than us for this same reason.

This doesn't mean we're all vindictive or voyeuristic at heart; however, it does invite us to explore who we are and who we've needed our friends to be (and they us) so we can step out of these confining roles together.

WHO'S ON MUTE?

Years ago, I was invited to do an interview online with someone I admire and respect. I was very excited and wrote out notes for my thoughts so I would be well prepared for the conversation. I made sure I got enough sleep and felt settled to show up for the call. Once I clicked on, however, I could hear them—but they couldn't hear me. I sprung into troubleshooting action. I muted and unmuted myself, tried different headphones, checked my computer microphone, left and rejoined the meeting, tried calling in from my phone, but nothing worked. Because I am dramatic and there's parts of me that feels the universe is out to get me, I felt defeated. Here was something I was so excited about, and now my computer audio wasn't working as if some invisible force was at work.

Then—suddenly, they said, "Oh! I can hear you. Haha, my volume was muted. Oops! Okay, well now we can get started!"

I was relieved. And also, frazzled. I had spent the last fifteen minutes becoming increasingly more anxious and frantic trying to figure out a problem that, as it turned out, wasn't on my end at all. While my escalating emotions were not the other person's responsibility, after the interview, I remember wondering what it would be like to not be worried or frantic in that moment—as they were. To not troubleshoot and just chill while a problem was being solved by someone else. I also wondered why I assumed it was my audio or problem without asking them to check anything on their end, letting my panic increase accordingly.

When I hear someone label a friend as dramatic, it reminds me of this moment. How often we assume the drama is the other person and that it's just their life until one day it's something we decide isn't "healthy" for us anymore. (Usually when we finally label them toxic and call it quits.) While that can be true, it's also continuing a pattern of a one-sided approach to friendship that we're simultaneously all participating in yet unaware we want out of. We may be worried we're the one on the stage and realize we're carrying more of the responsibility for failure or entertainment than we should.

PROJECTION, BUT IN A GOOD WAY

The psychology of what we're talking about here is called projection and how it shows up in friendship. Projection is where what we are afraid of in ourselves, we look for in others, typically so we can judge or blame them. This provides some relief because we spend our energy critiquing someone else rather than criticizing ourselves. If we need to preserve an idea of who we are to protect ourselves, we will use projection whenever that idea is threatened.

However you perceive yourself, a gentler approach to this concept is to consider how it applies to the positive labels we give our friends too. Like someone telling you you're the creative one or you saying they're better at something you actually know how to do and have an interest in too. The truth is, friendship is a place where we move close to our desires, and sometimes that's a scary thing to do because our goodness is far more vulnerable,[6] which might sound counterintuitive. We're conditioned to assume that our flaws are more threatening to our relationships, just like we are conditioned to people-please or stay small so others aren't uncomfortable. People who grow call us to grow, and if you're the friend showing up to big things in your life when your friend isn't, it can be startling to feel the distance between you expand as you step toward your desires. Sometimes we don't even know we are holding back on ourselves because we are unconsciously afraid of the potential to lose our community if we were to fully show up in our beauty.

This isn't always the case and of course we look for those who are brave enough to exhibit the gifts we hope to develop and acknowledge in ourselves in choosing people to befriend. This gives us a little breathing room through the playfulness of witnessing each other. We can see that it's safe to be good at something, to love what we love, and desire what we desire. It's the beautiful part of being in the audience, where those on the stage are in a relationship of mutual enjoyment with each other. This is one of the ways our friendships let us move from being a bystander to stepping onto the stage of our own lives. When we delight in the goodness of someone else, we move closer to belonging with each other, in addition to feeling more connection to similar goodness in ourselves (like my best friend's mom showing my mom how to homeschool). When we see that our friends have freedom in themselves in the same way that we long for and we accept the invitation to join them (and don't envy), it's because they've allowed us to witness their goodness and we've made the choice to move out of that front row seat of fear.

Though not in the category of compliments, drama is also one of the things we see in our friends, but not yet something we acknowledge as part of connection in friendship. This is partly because of what we've been told, and also because we continue to pretend drama is inherently wrong. When you think about the stories we were handed as children and the goal of every "happy" ending being a lifelong connection of wedded bliss, this makes sense. On the off chance a story didn't end this way, that person's friends were there for them to make up the difference. Now the messaging is to "drama-proof" our social life the same way we were advised to "divorce-proof" our marriages. And look how that turned out.

A FRESH NEW HELL TO PAY

Remember how we talked about the collective impact of the good-friend trope in the last chapter and how this freedom is happening for romance at the expense of friendship? This is where we can see the cost of that through the harsh (i.e., toxic) or comparative ("I outgrew them") labels that get dispensed on friends we've loved and lost. We need to engage what this looks like in our friendships on an individual level.

Essentially while being the good friend is the demand of the collective to fulfill our need of objectified connection leftover from redefining romance, labeling our friends as dramatic is our participation in that structure as individuals. The widespread othering that happens when there's drama is a symptom, showing that we still demand some version of perfection from one another, and if you can't provide that, then there's a fresh new performative hell to pay.

It's how we push people away when they don't show up to our expectation of happily ever after, while still having a story to watch that we can pretend we're not a part of.

WE DON'T NEED MORE INFORMATION

This is why we don't need more information on how to be better friends but rather, permission and freedom to be the bad friend if we truly want to make room for our full humanity in friendship. We've been trying to escape a desert of loneliness by being good. We are tired, and longing for life.

So, just like we wouldn't pick up a novel if it did not hold an element of some form of drama, we need to reclaim our desire for life in our friendships in the same way by moving closer to the stories where we ended up in the dramatic circumstances we've been told to distance ourselves from.

Esther Perel talks about this from the perspective of romantic partnerships, revealing how we can't ask one person to be everything for us, or be the one person to check every box on someone else's list of needs and desires.[7] This is good because it means we're acknowledging that we need each other in more ways than we realize, and we're learning to get specific about who can meet those needs, lifting the burden off one person to fulfill us . . . at least, romantically. Once we can realize this same truth applies in friendship, the next step is to recognize part of our humanness is a desire for intrigue and drama, allowing us to start enjoying our friendships in a new way because we've stopped demanding that they be perfect.

Much of the dialogue surrounding relationships could be explained as getting clear about our desires and needs, how we communicate those things, and who gets to be present with us in that vulnerable space. The problem is, we're operating on the assumption that we have been liberated from certain desires in friendship, when the reality is we're just unconsciously looking for them to be fulfilled.

It's actually the reason we're so invested in finding good friends and getting rid of toxic ones; we're investing in filling the roles left by our hopes and dreams for a fairytale romance . . . with friendships. What we don't plan for, because we aren't acknowledging this idealized view of who our friends will be for us, is when the fantasy of our friendship starts to fall apart. We already have the structures of blame in place when someone doesn't fit the BFF narrative we've all subliminally agreed on. This is where we get, or give, the *dramatic* label. Except, we can't selectively experience the goodness of friendship without knowing someone as a whole person. When we reject each other when things go south, it causes us to miss out on all the things that truly allow us to feel seen, connected, and alive.

The truth is that all this dynamic beauty, and more, is found through vulnerability in friendship. Which comes with risk and requires curiosity, maybe a little danger, and eventually some conflict. This is part of the pursuit of greater freedom and connection. When we are afraid of certain flaws in ourselves, or real goodness in another, we write it off as drama.

There is a reason each chapter of this book is centered around a story, and a name we give, or have given, a friend. When we search for a "forever" friend without realizing and do not find it, we protect ourselves by labeling it as something else. A friend we made hold our unconscious desire for a perfect lifelong relationship that fails us gets labeled by us. A friend who didn't play the part we wanted them to in our lives, or protect us from ourselves and others, gets written out of the story.

While it's easy to nod your head in resonance through every story that acknowledges a name you have been called, we still don't realize we limit ourselves by however we choose to define other people. It's our way of taking back power in a friendship where something unsettled us, without risking conflict or being clear about what we wanted, what hurt, and what we needed. It's an illusion of protection for our identity, a place where we tell ourselves we have taken the moral "high ground," when in reality, it requires us to also reject the parts of us that could ever be perceived that way by others. This means that for every dramatic friend we've written off, we live afraid of being the dramatic friend. All the while shutting down and locking away so much of ourselves in the process. The same goes for every other label we use against one another, and in so doing, we exile further and further away, deeply alive parts of who we are that are simply longing to be seen and connect.

My mother became a shell of herself the more she labeled and distanced herself from the life of her friend, and I watched her do it at the same time that my tender ten-year-old heart desperately wanted her to show me how to show up for my friend in a moment of unspeakable grief.

Who hasn't felt the invisible weight of shame from carrying the labels we feel we never would have received had we been a good-enough or better friend? The heaviness we carry around extends beyond the timeline of our adult friendships and further back into our young history than we want to acknowledge.

This way of seeing how we've labeled, or been labeled by others, flips the script on all of our friend breakup stories.

REFRAMES AND REFLECTIONS

One of the beautiful things about friendship is how they are a place where we mirror each other. We find people who are like us enough so we feel understood and yet unlike us so that we may discover more of who we are together. We speak adjectives and descriptors as compliments and delight: "She's funnier," "He's bolder," or "They're so passionate." And while these qualities belong to the friend we love, we are also drawn to them and honor them as the safe manifestation of hidden desires within ourselves. If we are not ready to be creative but we want to, we find a friend who is so. If our friend is not ready to take risks, they will watch us take them to learn what's possible. This is how in friendship we witness, we delight, we hope, we discover, and together, we become.

The reverse is also true. In our language, we find ways to move toward each other and our true selves, as well as farther apart. Yet these labels and their social definitions are currently held as black and white, good and bad. We call our friends, or ex-friends, the labels of things we don't want to be associated with or manage (like *toxic* or *dramatic*), without ever looking to see what this reveals about what we're afraid of in ourselves.

Like my story in Chapter One, you might want to reframe my label *clueless* as innocent or well-intentioned, calling one "bad" or the other "good," especially if you carry shame in a story of your own naivety. Or maybe you compensate by being the most informed, insightful, or attentive friend in your group . . . so you will never feel the weight of the label *clueless*. Except you get tired of being the one who always knows what to do or how to show up because you're living limited by the painful stories you carry.

Too often, our unseen and disappointed desires in friendship end with us defining the other person instead of engaging our friendship story with them as whole. While a label may lock the pain away, its simplification destroys what was once sacred, and the disconnection from ourselves will continue.

In many ways this is just the same formula of Prince Charming and happily-ever-after rebranded for friendship. Even the classic TV show *Friends* has a group of six individuals who somehow manage to stick together through a lot of genuinely concerning conflict. Any narrative we see around friendship shows people who always find a way to work through things but never offer a real exploration of the ways friendship confronts us with who we are, and sometimes that means you end up parting ways if you don't address your projections.

WHAT DOES IT MEAN TO BE ALIVE?

We are still playing into this idea that there is some way every-thing can work out in our friendship by checking all the boxes, except now it looks like: "become a boundaries queen," "12 ways to be a good friend," "cut toxic people out of your life," but also, "don't be afraid of vulnerability," "you are enough," and "we're all connected." Each one of these pieces of advice, and soon-to-be clichés, are in search of the same result of a happily-ever-after and an idealized vision of what belonging looks like. We don't know how to include the drama, so we maintain this fantasy, dismissing the unaccepted, unconsciously exiled, and arguably most human parts of ourselves. It works until it doesn't, and we are starting to feel how it's leaving us deeply unsatisfied.

The reason finding or having friendship feels complicated is because none of these standards account for the real beauty and drama it is to be alive. We're imagining a friend can simultaneously be good and exist without all the things that make for a beloved story while also making our friendships unconsciously hold the parts of the narrative we're too afraid to own as desires, or faults, in ourselves. And when that impossible equation doesn't balance out, we have a new system for discarding *failed* friendships.

We're unwilling to own the fullness of our desires and afraid to acknowledge the depth of our flaws. No wonder, we, and our friendships, are so tired.

When we don't acknowledge our hidden desires, we choose to experience pleasure by proxy, making friendship "safer" and easier to define when something difficult comes up, instead of recognizing there's a reflection of ourselves in them inherent to our connection with each other. When we keep shame and harm buried in our stories, we hand over the responsibility to tend to these parts of ourselves, making friendship our barometer for acceptance, allowing the person across from us to carry the burden of things we think we can't hold. This protects us when conflict comes up, giving us an exit door so we can leave them as the only one holding a flaw that is also ours to own.

This is not saying every person and every behavior is speaking to who you are or that you should offer your limited energy to always understanding and internalizing it. Rather, it is when you begin to see the friendships you have as something you invested in, for both a conscious and unconscious reason, that you will begin to see yourself and your friends differently as well as more fully.

That's the invitation held in learning how to be a dramatic friend. It means being the good friend is no longer a requirement, and that you and your friend get to be yourselves, to be human, to be alive.

A SLOW AND TENDER PROCESS

This is scary because it's similar to the media's influence on romance that friendships have the same narratives to contend with. Friends carry the burden of a unique stereotype when it comes to humanity's desire for forever, and just how much drama is socially permissible—or demanded. (See again: reality TV.) It's partly why a divorce or romantic breakup can be held by the community and yet no one knows how to hold space for the drama of a friend breakup. We're left floundering, our other friends don't know whose "side" to take, and most of the time, everyone just wants to find a way to relieve the tension, so we end up losing an entire community just from conflict with one person.

Romance is allowed to be dramatic, we are told, but heaven forbid our friendships are so complex and intricate.

Part of the awkwardness of this is that a friendship is so similar to a romance. But if you were to make a movie about two friends who broke up, you couldn't make it about their individual selves, it would be a single story (with one main and one secondary character) and even the parallel stories would still be about the friendship by nature of its absence. Unlike an unrequited love narrative where there's some relief in the simplicity of romance ending with phrases like, "Well, they just weren't the one" or "It wasn't meant to be," a friend breakup confronts us with the trauma of our undefined endings. They're not dead or in a romantic relationship with someone else, they are alive and well and still getting along with all their other people. In that is a particular loneliness we have yet to make room for. It's a loneliness where we are still connected to whomever we've lost, and moving through that is a slow and tender process.

The setup currently, for the bad friend or the broken-up-with friend, is to keep ourselves disconnected from such complex "drama," or if we find ourselves there, it's because of something we missed or did "wrong." All this actually does is keep us and our former friends from all the desires and hopes that created the friendship in the first place. This keeps us from being known in new ways within ourselves and with others, such that sometimes we break up with parts of ourselves when we break up with others, and those are usually the parts we are not ready to accept or reckon with.

When you look at it that way, you begin to see how we are all losing with the way we are approaching friendship and managing friend breakups. It's loss on top of loss, and to whose benefit? And again, why is this part of human connection not being talked about?

BROKEN HEART ISO: UNBROKEN TRUST

To reveal why we need the label of the dramatic friend, let's look back to our hidden desire for forever. Have you ever wondered what's underneath that? How maybe what we're really after is an unbroken heart? Even though we know in our minds that's not realistic and we like to pretend we're fine without it, the need persists, hidden in another form. Having weathered broken hearts from significant others, we demand friendship to maintain unbroken trust, with the threat of being labeled or outcast should we fail.

While we do talk about trust and rebuilding it and creating good things like boundaries, this discussion often avoids the way we hold others to an impossible standard without ever acknowledging our own failings. Once again, we have just moved one idea into a different box to be checked by a different person. We say "These are my boundaries" but rarely ask what our friend's are. The same as an unbroken heart requires us to live guarded from real intimacy is the desire for our idea of trust to be met through another person's performance in relationship with us and not the mutuality needed for true vulnerability.

Here is where the dramatic friend comes into play. Both of these desires require someone else to be deficient. Intellectually we could say, "Why yes, no one can please us and make us feel safe always—I know I couldn't!" But this does nothing for how we actually use and engage with people; that's what we do unconsciously. So, in order to trust a friend implicitly (who we know is just human), we might find another friend as a placeholder for any suspicion, or to manage life in a lifeless marriage, or we have a friend who's always on the rebound to keep things entertaining, and we may not even realize it! We just know that in some way, their story holds something we don't want to be true about ourselves. In return for our connection, they keep what we don't want to know about ourselves, safe and manageable. Just like my mother who found a friend living the life she longed for without taking any of the risk to own those desires in herself.

We need the dramatic friend, so we can pretend we aren't involved in it, so we can stay safe and a little less alive. The contrast of our lives with theirs makes our lack of drama possible and protects us from ever becoming that ourselves because we literally form our identity out of fear of becoming like "them." Never acknowledging that our friendship with them tells us something about who we wish we could be.

HOW WE PAY FOR CONNECTION

Here's another friendship example for you from my life. I love fashion, I love spending money, I love shopping. All of these things are fun to me, they are interesting, and I'm actually quite good at it. While I love a good deal, I also love finding the perfect piece and buying it at full price.

I used to have two friends who were on specific budgets for different reasons. They also both liked fashion, shopping, finding deals, and spending money—just in different ways.

They would make comments about my spending, somewhat playfully, but it made me insecure enough to make excuses to seek their approval. I responded by regularly complimenting their frugality, or, through small actions—like picking up the tab, and buying their coffees when we went out. We agreed on roles to play based on what we wanted to feel. They didn't want to feel the lack that their chosen budgets required, so they'd criticize my spending. I didn't want to feel the shame of being called a "spender" so I'd compliment their lifestyle and, basically, paid for the pleasure of their company.

This same concept plays out emotionally too. Our dramatic friends pick up the tab for the emotions we don't want to feel, or acknowledge we have. We watch them ride the rollercoaster of life and get enough out of it without having to be on the ride ourselves. If we don't feel safe to say what we don't like about our lives, we'll find someone who "complains"; and we can experience complaining without having to take responsibility for it—or feel the need to change our lives because we are dissatisfied with it.

Are all such relationships like this "negative"? Yes and no—what I want you to see through the stories in this book is that all our definitions and the names we have been called in past friendships invite us to belong. To be the [fill in the blank] friend you are in a way that fully expresses who you are and what you desire is part of being alive and what you and your friend will discover about yourselves in connection to each other. This, in essence, is to be human together.

WHERE ACCEPTANCE STARTS

Before you start to ask yourself, "What is it I want?" or "What are my unconscious desires?" or "Which kind of friend am I?" or "Onto which friends am I projecting?" or "Which friends are projecting on to me?" first simply ask: What are the stories you love? What are the conflicts you find in the books you love to read?

What tropes or plot lines are you drawn to, and where have you felt tension or uncertainty in your life? Which characters do you love to love, or love to hate? If you were to cast your friendships as roles in the story, who would they be and who do you see yourself to be with them? What traits do your friends have that you wish you did? What flaws do they accept in themselves that you cannot have grace for in yourself? Notice how they express a part of you in some way. This is how you begin to turn your gaze to your stories in friendships: notice the ways the stories you love and the people who you love bring an unfolding drama to your life that's meant to be enjoyed.

These questions, "What do you need more of?" or "Who do you desire to be?" are just as important as "What are you not allowed to feel that feels like too much?"

The freedom in discovering the answers to these questions is that you can then go and find humans who have what you need—not so you can get it from them, but so you can begin to allow yourself to need that too. You can find friends who are whom you desire to be, not so you can imitate, but so you can find within yourself the freedom to become more alive. And then, look tenderly and notice your friends who express or own in themselves faults that you're afraid of—not so you can judge but so you can begin to untangle yourself from the narrative of shame that has bound us all up for so long: the toxic fairytale that says good friends are not a part of a story that has conflict or drama or endings.

We need other people because as we learn to be with each other, we discover ourselves. We need reflection of the entirety of who we are, "the good, the bad, and the ugly" as they say. Our hunger for this in friendship is found in the questions that play on repeat in our heads, such as: "Am I too much? If I think my friend is over-the-top, does that mean I can't take up more space?" We stop ourselves short of being fully seen because the roles we've had to take on are so ingrained there's no room for anything else. Not only does this hurt, but it keeps us isolated from each other. Even the "too much" friend may feel like they have to put on a show because they aren't allowed to be calm. It's a merry-go-round we never wanted to be on, and I believe we are all ready to get off.

This is where acceptance starts and what kindness truly looks like. It is a willingness to know our own story and all the roles we not only have been asked to play but also those we've cast others into. It's not to say these roles aren't real, and perhaps even necessary, but do they belong to you? How can the titles, labels, and characters you've been given become your own?

I wouldn't be writing a book like this if I wasn't a little bit dramatic; it's just that now it belongs to me as a part of what I give and receive in a relationship rather than something that is used against me. I no longer believe my emotions mean I'm deserving of pity and neither do yours. I'm a dramatic friend, maybe you are too, and depending on the story you're writing, I might be good or bad until you realize that happiness forever isn't what we are really after. What we want is to belong, to be alive, and to be seen as fully ourselves, which isn't measured by the length of a relationship. We want to be with others in their lives through all that is "beautiful and terrible"[8] and to be able to look at each other and say, "I'm not afraid."

So embrace the drama, conflict, and beauty you and your friendships have been a part of, knowing that if you do, just like every good story, things get a little bit complicated, messy, and . . . *difficult*.

CHAPTER FOUR

HOW TO BE A DIFFICULT FRIEND

"It is the quality of your relationships which ultimately will determine the quality of your [life]."

—Esther Perel[1]

"Significant conflict is required for growth."

—Dr. Dan Allender[2]

Some things in life are just difficult, and it helps when there's someone there to navigate them with us. Traveling and renting a car is one of them.

Allow me to be of service.

If you're planning a trip to the UK (or Ireland) in the near future, before you decide to rent a car, there's a few things you need to know.

1) Driving a car in another country is fun.

2) The car will not be $9 a day as is advertised.[3] It will be at least $30 a day more, or require a $3K–$5K hold on your credit card or bank account.

3) While your car insurance will cover any damages, and often a credit card company will too, the rental agency will accept neither of these in place of the added insurance or hold.

4) Purchasing the insurance provided by the online booking will be less expensive but it is also not accepted by the rental agency. Even though the online booking company will say so online.

5) The hold will be released on your credit card five to eight days after you return the car with no damages.

6) Most cars in the UK or Ireland are manual.

7) Driving a manual car in the UK or Ireland is very, very fun.

Most of these things I learned on a single trip to The Republic of Ireland with my partner. Except for the first one that I've known since I was ten, when I learned how to shift gears while sitting in the passenger seat of a rental car in the UK.

The tip on the online insurance was something I learned trying to circumvent the inconvenience of all the other restrictions when planning a trip abroad with friends. I knew I wanted to rent a car, because we were traveling together to an event with a few days to spare afterward. I asked them what they thought and we all agreed it would be more fun than a bus tour, plus one of them wanted to try driving there too. I got everything figured out and I was very excited. Until the day came to pick up the car.

This was going to be my first trip abroad on my own, which is important to note because I became a mother very young as a product of the cult-ish homeschooling environment I was raised in.

While my family and I had since moved away, I had not known the freedom of being on my own—ever in my life—and so the adventure of the open road in another country was calling to me as a place of courage, healing, and delight. I couldn't wait. I learned how to drive a manual in high school (thank goodness), and I was ready to embrace the new challenge of a right-hand manual drive in the beautiful green countryside along with some beautiful friends.

We make allowance for different kinds of difficulty in the world, difficult things like traveling and renting a car, or difficult people in our lives, but things get tricky when difficulty shows up in our close friendships. There are certain things we expect to be difficult, like running a marathon, going to the DMV, or learning a new skill, and then there are other things we tell ourselves aren't difficult, or shouldn't be, if we are doing it "the right way."

Tolerance and patience pair well with difficulty. Especially when it comes to the kind of difficult things we manage while dealing with family on holidays or a colleague we disagree with. We take a deep breath and find a way to get through it in the hopes of making things easier, often because we simply aren't holding any hope of being seen and known in these contexts; and for those of us who are survivors of abuse, it's quite a thing to discover that relationships can be *easy*—to realize we don't have to numb ourselves in order to survive being around someone who won't compromise or just wants to be miserable.

So when Esther Perel says, "The quality of your relationships . . . determines the quality of your [life],"[4] it can be startling. We start to notice how we've separated our life from so many relationships (like work and family) in order to stay sane and survive.

If what Esther says resonates with us to where we want change, we notice ourselves combing through our lives and hearts, wondering, *What are the qualities that contribute to a high-quality relationship? What are the qualities I want in my life?*

My guess would be that if you made a list, *difficult* would not be one of them. In fact, it's probably something you'd be afraid to find in yourself or others, something that would threaten a sense of belonging or acceptance, especially when it comes to friendship, a relationship that by its very nature is sparked by similarity, synchronicity, and shared experience.

THE QUALITIES WE WANT

C. S. Lewis describes friendship as the moment someone says, "What? You too? I thought I was the only one."[5] So if we're making a list of qualities that contribute to a relationship that reflects the life we want, we might put down *curious, playful, easy.* All of which are lovely things.

Now, let's think of things that are more like opposites: stubborn, intense, complicated. Which list do you want your life to be like, which list would you rather be friends with? All of us would pick the first one; in fact, I think many of us have experience with the second, and as a result we are trying to make our relationships more reflective of our desires when it comes to life and connection.

The trouble is, though, being a person includes both. Even the same friendship (over time or not) may swing back and forth between the two, rather than simply being one or the other. We might acknowledge this as obvious about any relationship, because isn't that what we want for ourselves? The freedom to not have to be judged in relationships on if we are easygoing enough or not?

Take a moment to consider, what do you define as difficult in a person? How do you define *easy*? Have you ever consciously thought about it? And is it the same, or different, for what you hope others make allowance for in yourself? Or do you have a difficult friend that manifests, as we discussed in the previous chapter, the supposed negative difficult traits you're afraid of seeing in yourself?

I've observed that as a whole, our unspoken idea of a high-quality (a.k.a. a "good") friendship is someone who sees what we need, can meet what we need, and doesn't appear to have any themselves—which by that we mean, doesn't have needs or desires in conflict with our own. We see things that tell us what good friends look like or how we can be more like that to our friends instead of engaging the fact that being a human is hard, and that makes us difficult sometimes. Not only that, but by embracing our values, purpose, and desires, we become more "difficult" to the friends who once described us as easygoing.

While we applaud and commemorate and celebritize difficult people in history (particularly difficult women), we discard them as our friends. This arises from the tension of feeling our desire but staying committed to the safety of being in the audience. We want the fulfillment of being on the stage without losing the power it gives us to be a critic. Put another way, we have seen the way difficult people were treated in their lifetime, and we question if our desires are worth it—except that means we need everyone else to stay small too. We can't bear both knowing what we want and the pain of holding back from it because we are afraid it will label us as difficult.

A writer and trail worker, Ana Maria Spagna captures this dissonance well in an essay on writing. She reflects on the similarities—but very distinct differences—between her and Cheryl Strayed: namely, fame and the desire for it. You've probably never heard of Ana; she knows that and confronts her desire to be seen in the wake of Cheryl's success with *Wild*. Articulating the space between those who show up to what they want in their life and those who hate them for it, saying, "It's not jealousy of success so much as the near-outrage we feel toward anyone who knows, even for a short time, exactly what she wants, and turns herself, as they say, body-and-soul to the task."[6]

This sentence has captured me since the moment I read it years ago. When we step into knowing what we want, be that friendship or anything else, "body and soul,"[7] we are confronted by those who will leave precisely because we are showing up. Which is when we will find ourselves being labeled difficult.

EIGHT TIMES AS LONG

When I went to Ireland, I was traveling with my partner. We found childcare rather last minute and booked the trip without very much research or preparation. I had been to the UK as a child, so even though I am an anxious traveler by nature, it felt easier because the experience was similar. I was surprised to see rental cars (and lodging) were not that expensive, and because we were using credit card miles to get there, the vacation was actually affordable to us at the time. We arrived jet-lagged and got a bus from the airport to the car rental place, which is where we learned we either had to pay a crazy additional amount per day (there went our trip's budget) or put a five thousand dollar hold on our credit card. First of all, we weren't even sure if that was over our limit, and we spent hours in the rental lobby with our phones plugged into the wall on 2G Wi-Fi researching what to do along with any other options.

What I've since learned about traveling anywhere—particularly for the first time—is that everything is just going to take a long time. In the book, *Deep Survival*, Laurence Gonzales shares two rules of life, the second of which is, *"Everything takes eight times as long as it's supposed to."*[8] I've never read anything that's felt more true of human existence, especially in that moment sitting in the rental car agency in Ireland. Something as small as how long it takes to solve a problem, understand a concept, or complete a task can increase our anxiety. Part of this is because we live in a world that favors those who are quicker, faster, smarter, etc., and part of this is because we might have been left out or behind if we couldn't "keep up."

It's the easiest thing in the world to get anxious the longer we spend time in a place, or feeling, that's unfamiliar, and then even easier to get frustrated with the person next to you in it, especially when you thought you had everything figured out only to hit another roadblock. If we don't have the main ingredient of time to spare, investing in a relationship or situation that is difficult probably won't feel worth it—unless we have an experience where it was to bank on.

After hours of trying to find a solution, my partner and I ended up opting for the hold and hoping we had enough cash to get through our trip. Once we got over the anxiety of basically owning this little rental car should anything happen to it, we had a really fun time. Did you know that gas stations in Ireland are just lovely?

The cheese you can buy there is better than anything you've ever had in the US. It's little stuff like that I'm so glad we didn't miss out on that made pushing through the difficulty of getting the car worth it.

This is the magic and the unexpected I was so thrilled to experience with my friends on our trip across the pond.

When I suggested renting a car could be fun—and they agreed—I took on the job of reserving one for all of us. While I would have rented a car either way, because there were places I wanted to see that you could only reach by car, my other friend was also interested in driving and it looked easy to add a second driver. I had done some more research after getting home from the last trip and thought I had found a way around all the crazy fees and credit card holds. It wasn't until the day we reserved to pick up our car, that I realized I hadn't.

Discouraged, I spent an hour on the phone with the agency while everyone else was doing their own thing. It felt like the entire decision process my friends and I had gone through to choose to rent the car basically had to be re-negotiated. Everything was taking "eight times as long as it [was] supposed to"[9] take, and I was running back and forth to where my friends were sitting and where I had a few bars of cell service letting them know things like "It is going to be double the cost to add a second driver, did you still want to do that?" And on and on. It was exhausting and I was frustrated, to say the least.

A few things happened in succession that, obviously in hindsight, I (and I think also they) would have handled differently. When I finally sorted things out with the agency, my friends didn't think they were coming with me to get the car (we had to pay for a taxi to and from). This startled me, and I began to feel the resentment I didn't know I was hiding bubble up inside me. If they wanted a car too and I was doing all the work, why weren't they willing to come with so I could have an extra person to help navigate as I was driving the car back to the hotel—at least for the first time?

Already annoyed at this point from all the time on the phone, I convinced them to come with, but by the time we got there, it turned out the solution the rental company promised me on the phone wasn't a real solution. They said they would look at the paperwork I had for the insurance I purchased online, which was probably just to get me in the door.

As you by now know, I had not, in fact, found a way around the hold. Except now when my friends heard the hold limit, their eyes got wide and they immediately wanted to bail and just find a bus tour, whereas I had become even more determined to rent the car after spending so many hours figuring it out along with weeks of anticipation. It was the same cost for one bus ticket as it was for all of us to split to rent the car, and I didn't want to see the countryside on a bus.

I told them that I was fine and that they could go on a bus, but I was still going to rent the car. Well, to be honest, what I actually said was I was still going "to rent the fucking car."

They said that was "not an option" and that they wanted us to stay together.

I repeated that I wanted to rent the car. For me, the only one with little kids and a family, it was a once-in-a-lifetime moment. I had made this choice weeks ago when I booked the trip. I hated the feeling in my body that my friends and I were no longer in agreement, but I hated even more the idea of what it would feel like in my body to relinquish this desire and get on a bus. I couldn't do it to myself. So I said no, again, and that they did not have to rent the car with me and that I could drop them off at a bus station.

There it was. I was a difficult friend. I didn't want to compromise. I had figured everything out, and it had taken me hours to that point in the day to finally get the keys.

Don't get me wrong, I was nervous about driving—and potentially alone but in the way I wanted to be, aside from the newly heightened tension of my friends wanting to back out of the process.

They looked at me like the crazed person I felt I was, the kind of look you see on someone's face trying to calm a dog that's getting aggressive. For a split second, I considered solving what they were feeling and changing how they were experiencing me. All I had to do was give up the car, and in that moment, I knew what this decision of mine was going to mean. I saw both paths clearly, with only one that would keep the friendships, and I let that one go.

I signed the paperwork, I took on the liability, the rental car agent who had been watching this drama unfold in the lobby handed me the keys, and then I got behind the wheel and drove. One friend sat in shotgun and graciously navigated us back to the hotel and through our travels the next three days, my other friend sat silently in the back seat with no commentary. A silence that spoke more loudly than if she had chosen to say something.

I only stalled once the whole time over three days of driving. Parallel parking was the dicey part and they both jumped out to help in that tough moment. And they—well, I—had a marvelous time. Had they not been with me, I would have struggled to see the map and probably would have gotten lost but eventually would have figured it out. I chose to tell myself the story that I could rebuild their trust and repair the friendship with good driving, showing that their fears in the rental agency were unfounded by proving my competence. I knew that wasn't true, they knew that wasn't true. The way I would have felt sitting on the bus is probably how they felt sitting in the car. Even now it brings up tension in me, which is one of the reasons I don't like to look at this story. I hate that my decision is the force in this story and the driving factor for all that happened next.

But when I think about how I felt in that lobby and what it would have meant for me to sit on a bus, I love that a people-pleasing girl who had been told to give up on her desires and had been taking care of children since she was eleven years old, managing the depression and anxiety that came with it, did not say no to herself again in that moment—even though it cost her connection in the process.

This doesn't change the fact that in being a difficult friend, I harmed my friends. That's not always the case when we are difficult, but it is in this one. Yet, in being the difficult friend, a part of me had the opportunity to choose herself in a way she never got to before.

Both are true. They don't cancel each other out or give the ugly one a silver lining.

And that's difficult to hold.

MESS OF OUR OWN MAKING

Interestingly, out of all the stories you'll read here, this one comes after almost every other one in this book. The reason how to be a difficult friend is here first is because, if you're going to begin to understand the desires and projections you hold unconsciously in your friendships, you're probably going to begin to know yourself in a new way, and you're going to start to be difficult.

In the past, I would never have rented the car (or traveled alone internationally) in the first place. I wouldn't have led the charge to drive the car, come hell or high water, and would have noticed their discomfort long before I even knew I wanted to drive in the UK again. Instead, I showed up differently to change the quality of my life, whereas before I would have only invited shared space and adventure insofar as I could guarantee someone else's positive feedback on the experience. Other people having a good time was my job, and I had spent my whole life losing myself in that process.

It was a messy moment, mostly of my own making, but also of people not showing up for themselves and either avoiding conflict or not taking responsibility to say no when they needed to. The lie about having to be easygoing or assuming our friendships should not be difficult is that those are the exact moments where things can be seen and held in ways we are capable of, we just don't know it yet.

In that rental agency, my desires and unwillingness to compromise meant my decision decided for my friends. Their desire for us to stay together and no longer rent the car put them in a bind of losing out on one of the things they wanted. It's important to address before I go on that my friends did stay in the difficulty of what happened (they got in the car after all) and both initiated conversations with me to follow up in expressing how they felt. Neither of these conversations resolved what happened that day, but too often we measure the success of our engagement by how much of the conflict feels resolved instead of honoring our attempts at reconnecting with each other. This is what happens when we are difficult, or choices are made that compromise our agency and needs. The question is, will we risk further attempts to let ourselves be seen by each other in how we felt about what happened?

Both of my friends leaned into the discomfort of the conflict renting the car had brought about. One of these conversations happened after the trip with the friend who rode shotgun. I was grateful she risked bringing it up and to hear it at a time when I could listen about her experience of me and how I impacted her that day.

The other conversation happened the last night of the trip when I was low on sleep and still emotionally charged about the whole situation. I was caught up in my desires for freedom and re-enacting failed friendship stories in a way I'll share more about in later chapters. My other friend was much older, and although I felt we related as peers, she had more than a few words for me about who she felt I was, which put me on the defensive.

RE-ENACTMENT

Remember how we talked in the last chapter about *The Lord of the Rings* and the roles we all play in each other's lives? Well, at this moment in my life, I was learning who I was going to be, and I noticed I was drawn to people who were in the same space from whom I assumed the same self-awareness. One of the roles I'm very aware that I play is that of the scapegoat. I am intense, and my intensity impacts people in different ways, and scapegoating is one of the common responses to that impact. I've since learned the ways I create that reaction, the same way I've learned that people are also responsible for how they respond—regardless of someone else's behavior. We have to own our own stories and understand the ways we are *re-enacting* them with each other instead of *being with* each other.

Here's what that means. We all have stories we tell ourselves about who we are that arise from—most often—our childhood. These usually have a pattern to them, the way things typically went down in your home growing up, and those patterns shape the way we see ourselves and the people we are in connection with in the present. Did you "always get in trouble"? Or could you "always talk your way out of it"? Did keeping your feelings to yourself keep you safe? Or was your anger regularly provoked so others could humiliate you as being "too emotional"? There are an infinite number of ways our history conditioned us to believe how relationships worked. This results in part of us remaining deeply committed to the old narrative in order to keep us safe, and another part of us that is always looking for a way out. We are always unconsciously seeking ways to confirm or deny what we were told was true about ourselves in these stories, or what is true about how people will interact with us as a result. While this is rooted in our attachment style, which we will get into in the next chapter, the word for what happens when we are in emotionally charged moments like this, such as conflict, is called re-enactment.

Re-enactment is a moment that replays a dynamic from your history through how people interact with you or you with them.[10] It's distinct from a trigger because a trigger is a personal thing; re-enactment happens in our interaction with others. Something important for you to understand is that it is *going* to happen. It's not a matter of you "healing enough" for it to not happen. The question of whether you've been cared for enough and if someone has named well what's happened in your story is what's going to determine what happens next—once the re-enactment has occurred or is occurring.

The other thing you need to know about re-enactment is that you can't think your way out of it. The awareness of it is going to come from your body because your body holds the memories of these encounters as well as the sense that it's happening again. So, what does this all mean? When we're not aware of re-enactment, it is a source of harm either for us because we're experiencing retraumatization, or *from* us with others because we're participating in their re-enactment and retraumatizing them. Sounds like a nightmare, right? But hang on because here is where it gets really cool.

When we are aware of re-enactment and we have the courage to name it, the replaying of our story actually becomes an opportunity for healing for both you and the other person. This is one of the opportunities presented to us in difficult friendships.

Re-enactment brings out the parts of us that learned to survive abuse; these are protective parts of ourselves. These parts of us also tend to have very limiting beliefs about how worthy we are of love. When we encounter conflict in friendship, it's like we get zapped back in time to those roles we played in our family. Part of how we kept ourselves safe, if that environment was harmful, is that we learned to know our enemy very well. What happens when we are no longer in that environment but haven't healed those stories is that our brain plays a trick on us and turns the friend we are fighting with into the person who did us harm. This takes us out of the conflict we are actually in and sets us up to where we are waiting on (and sometimes baiting) them to react to us in the same way.[11] Instead of being present to what is happening in the conversation, we are only taking in data that confirms our beliefs about ourselves and our powerlessness; instead of stepping into a new story when it comes to having conflict with others.

When I am in a conflict or argument, the role I am both committed to and looking for a way out of is that of the scapegoat, which means the parts of me that are trauma responses are always looking for someone who is blaming me (confirming my story) or willing to be accountable (rewriting my story). This is one of the ways I am pulled to re-enact my story that impacts my relationships if I, or those who love, me don't name that cycle when it's happening. The complex thing about this is that while we will re-enact in our friendships, we are also not responsible to change the story for our friends. In fact, if we get too invested in making sure we don't re-enact, we are going to miss our own needs even further in a difficult situation. Can you see how confusing and messy and icky this is starting to get? No wonder we abdicate what we desire in order to "keep the peace" and stay out of conflict.

There is so much more nuance and complexity to this, and any confrontation with a friend, but let's return to the role of the scapegoat, which is deeply connected to the label of *difficult* when it comes to friendship and our stories.

"A KID WITH SHIT TO PROVE"

Being a scapegoat means that you are the easy or willing target for what other people do not want to look at in themselves—or hold the right people responsible for. Many friendships exist in this "one-sided" reciprocity. This is where one friend does the things, or plans the things, or offers the things. By this, I mean the friend who makes decisions, openly shares their failures, or takes the risk to reveal their opinion is often paired with a friend who goes along with it (like the silent observer of the last chapter)—until they decide that isn't working for them anymore.

In the case of my friendship with the woman who chose to sit in the back seat, I felt the familiarity of my role as a scapegoat when she broached the conversation about her discomfort in the car on the final night of our trip. She ordered a bottle of wine and started talking to me about how she did not approve of my decision to rent the car, continuing on to remark about my driving and having to "bounce around in the back seat." When I asked her why she hadn't sat up front, she said she and my other friend had agreed because of my "attitude" that it would be better for her to sit back there because she didn't think I would listen to her directions. I felt a seething rage of resentment creep into my chest in the kind of way that makes you frighteningly calm. Even to write about it now, I feel it. The parts of me that sought to confirm my story won out in this encounter. She went on to tell me I was a "just a kid with shit to prove" and that "my energy in the rental agency was bad," referring to me as a "hurricane."

I felt reprimanded, punished as if I was a child. Knowing I was the same age as some of her children and that she had bemoaned to me her own children's unwillingness to listen to her, I leveraged that with equal cruelty to try and escape the pain I felt from her words. Was I just the captive audience she hadn't gotten elsewhere to speak her truth about how she hadn't felt heard in her life? I told myself my intentions were good, but I watched as what I said cut deeply. In the moment, I felt the defiance of refusing her projections of me. In this moment, I can clearly name the weight of my resentment of her and that this, not my good intentions, was how I struck back. The tension in the rental agency was too much to simply allow either of us to have a conflict about the car, and it led to re-enactment which ended in more harm to us both. Had this been acknowledged or had the conversation made it through the woods of confusion into a place of unknown but new understandings, things might have been different. I know I had an illusion of my own integrity when I thought it could be so.

Instead, when I said no to owning her interpretation of me by asking if this really had something to do with an issue with me or with something in her own life, she physically got up and walked away. If I'm honest, I wish I had too. In a funny way, she was right. I was a kid with shit to prove, just not about the rental car. I became the scapegoat in the conflict loop of my own story where I learned to fight it out as a child because I wasn't allowed to walk away.

Conflicts are interesting in this way because we are not usually taught how to have them. Let me clarify, we are taught indirectly, but not led, shown, and given language so we are equipped to offer empathy to ourselves and others. It makes sense to me that so many people hate conflict and our idea of "easy" runs around relationships that don't have it. The amount of gaslighting and abuse most people have suffered works in two ways to keep us from the idea that tension is essential to the well-being of every relationship, even among friends.

In our story, harm often teaches us that conflict is something to be afraid of and is, in fact, the indicator that further harm is coming because the "conflict" only arises when we (the victim) have been "unable" to keep the peace. The second way it works as survivors of abuse is when we do get to have normal relationships that are easy, we are so used to managing our abuser to make things work that we assume we are a failure if we bring conflict to our new relationships. When it's only been our job to keep the peace, if there's a problem, we often need the other person to be the problem because we are used to being the victim in harmful relationships.

Enter the difficult friend. If someone knows their mind, stands their ground, and communicates clearly with you, but you have not addressed your history of harmful, demanding, and likely abusive parents, partners, or even friends, their assertiveness will feel *bad* to you. It will set off all your fire alarms, and while you possess enough self-awareness to know what's happening means something is problematic, it may not be enough to recognize that the person in front of you is not solely responsible for the harm (especially if you haven't done the healing work to hold your abuser accountable). Every instinct and action from you will be to target the person who is most willing and available to actually, and authentically, engage you.

In feeling like a child, and being referred to as one, I stood up for myself in the conflict with my friend in a way I wish I had with the people who harmed me. I can't say for certain, but it felt like some of her words came from that place for her too.

When you're with someone you want to label as difficult, you are probably witnessing someone holding to themselves in a way you wish you were, which is why it is so triggering to anyone who has had to abandon themselves to survive. It will feel foreign, and like my friend who confronted me as the difficult friend, you might need to walk away.

We didn't speak again. She made a cruel off-hand comment to me at a mutual gathering, then messaged me a week later asking to meet for coffee. I didn't respond to her invitation for coffee, not because I'm unwilling to work things out, but I've realized what it means for both of us to be ready and that it's okay for a friendship to end. I wish she hadn't run away that evening, I still wonder the "what if" of having said something differently, and yet, I showed up as true to who I was in that moment as I could, resentment included, after spending many years compromising myself to put other people at ease. It was difficult. I was difficult. This story is difficult.

DWELL IN COMPLEXITY

Sometimes I think we sabotage so we don't have to suffer. Bail on the conversation, call someone names, leave a snide comment. What that really means is, we still experience pain, we just want it to be predictable. Uncertain pain, the pain of healing, of leaning into difficulty and owning our own difficulty in the process is unknown, unfamiliar, and agonizing.

You could say I was a jerk about the car, and you're not wrong, I was. At the same time I also was ready to accept my friends regardless of whether they wanted to go buy a bus ticket or not. I was on a personal quest inviting others along, but wouldn't bend the destination in order to soothe someone else's anxieties anymore, which were lingering projections from my own story.

My understanding of how I'm a difficult friend continues to change and evolve through the years. I know for that moment in the rental car lobby, I was healing by standing up for myself and what I actually wanted. I'd been clear about my plans and intentions with plenty of warning. I was also still in the wounding of my own story. I didn't trust that we'd all have a good time because after a lifetime of compromising, I'd never experienced the difficulty of a change in plans that included my desires and joy as well. Think of Alyssa and the lip sync contest. I had to give up the song I wanted to do because someone else didn't want to go with me. This time I made a choice to cling to what I felt I needed and wanted in that moment, at the expense of these friendships.

There are threads of our stories that run through us like that. We find ourselves in situations that re-enact or rewrite, especially when we lean into what we want for ourselves and we let our friends see that. It is both healing and hard, healing because there is something new on the other side of saying yes to ourselves, hard because there isn't always resolution for the times spent in conflict with someone else. When we don't label someone, it does leave us without a neat little bow that explains away the pain of what happened. There isn't resolution for this story either, and that's part of why losing friends is difficult and being difficult may cost you friends.

It is easier to tell ourselves this isn't a quality we want in our friends, but that also means we will miss out on so much beauty, adventure, and growth.

To be difficult is to be resilient, determined, aware, all beautiful things that we need for ourselves and that are a gift to bring each other. Emily Dickinson says, "I dwell in Possibility—"[12] and I feel a similar line might be, "I dwell in complexity." Someone who is hard to please, or understand, has more to their story than just our impression of them. You have more to your story than any of your friends will ever know. Perhaps some will wander the maze of your mind and life with you for a while. But if and when they leave or if and when you need to, don't simplify the singular experience of their whole being into "one of *those* people," or you'll live afraid of becoming the difficult person yourself.

Sometimes we need difficult people, because they protect us from the obstacles in ourselves we don't want to wrestle with. It's more familiar for us to write someone off or run away from a real conversation. When we do that though, we miss the opportunity to remove the obstacle protected by our simplistic impression of them. Even though the obstacle is costing us in ways we don't realize are impacting the quality of our life. In keeping our idea of who someone is rather than becoming curious to understand them for who they are, we keep everyone in the set role that will continue to re-enact old stories. *Difficult* is a word you have with a meaning inside your mind defining a world inside them that you are invited to be curious about and explore. Same goes for yourself. The people you think of as difficult—the ones you think of when you see a meme or were told by others you didn't have to "like" but "love"—these are the people who will challenge and change your narrative.

You can live with absolutes for only as long as your experience stays within the roles you learned long ago were there to be played. Sometimes life and friendships and things are complicated and you should walk the other way. Sometimes they are complex and a difficult friend is no different from a plot twist in the story. That label is an easy way to dismiss what's really a difficult decision to stay and lean in, or walk away. I hope you choose to lean in sometimes and walk away in others, and that you risk both ending and beginning friendships with people who do not think like you, but not because of needing to fix the difference between you but the newness that difference invites you to.

We don't realize how much we are actually longing for and needing people in our lives who are so connected to themselves that it startles us. We need to start acknowledging the difficult person in front us may, in fact, be someone who belongs to themselves. We do not think they are good, because they aren't giving us what we need/want or are not compromising what they need/want in order to show up for us. This doesn't change the fact that these are exactly the kinds of things we wish we were brave enough to do. And in a world raised as a generation of people-pleasers, by mothers who were told to be martyrs, our idea of who we should be was largely shaped by how the adults in our life behaved and what they demanded of us in the process, and then we look for our friends to fill that gap.

While two people who love and belong to themselves are able to build trust with each other, that doesn't mean things are always easy. This kind of relationship will mean they will eventually encounter difficulty together. The invitation out of the re-enactment in that moment will look like creatively finding a way to come to an agreement, or allowing the difference and consequences of it to exist between them amicably with or without resolution.

We romanticize the idea of self-love and self-belonging, acting as if once we are in friendships with people connected to themselves that we will have some sort of difficulty-free happily-ever-after. This fails to address the very real needs we have as humans that will eventually involve conflict and difficulty, both of which will occur precisely *because* we are connected to ourselves and what we desire.

We can't hold on to the idea of "how a good friend shows up for you" and the idea that other people are difficult when they set boundaries or don't want to compromise. The truth is, difficult women are connected to their bodies and selves. The only reason we learned to call them difficult is because the conformity demanded of women in a social construct requires them to deny all their needs and desires in exchange for "love" and safety.

Difficult becomes a reality in our friendships when compromise is not a solution, particularly when compromise involves a departure from ourselves to where it is not authentic. This is the fawn response, which we learned from demanding narcissists and gaslighters who required us to buy into their narrative or experience harm without protest.

Passing this burden and wounding off to our friends who don't agree with what we want to do is missing out on the gift that difficulty in friendship means to us.

When we meet someone connected to themselves to the point where you can trust them when they say yes or no or "I can (or can't) make that work," the friend who you can call because you know they won't pick up the phone unless they are available, the person you can trust not to overextend themselves and who is actually having a good time—these are the people who are not afraid to be difficult (i.e. be themselves with you).

If we want to overcome the difficulties in our lives, and we know we can't do that alone, then we need to familiarize ourselves with our desires in friendship and be willing to get uncomfortable holding them even in a space of disagreement with our friends.

These moments actually become the training ground of resiliency that invites us to become more clear about who we are, how we want to show up, and where we need to grow.

This freedom is found in realizing you are not required to be easy, or good, in fact you can't be if you're going to show up for your desires. We are afraid of being seen as difficult because the label was intended to haunt us when we reach for our desires or own our needs. Being difficult might be something you brazenly own and pretend you've never lost out on as a result, but the truth is, you have. We all have, and if we fail to acknowledge the very real cost any of these failed attempts at staying connected to ourselves in a friendship have meant, we are in just as much of a fantasy.

The underlying accusation that stings more than *difficult* hits directly at the place we need to love and are trying to connect with as we heal from the loss of friendships: our self. Once we know what we desire, and we show up to it "body and soul,"[13] ready to write a new story, we also let go of the perfectionism that's masked as selflessness, leading us to reckon with the title of being a selfish friend.

CHAPTER FIVE

HOW TO BE A SELFISH FRIEND

"Are You My Mother?"

—P. D. Eastman[1]

Boundaries is a hot-button word. We hear it a lot. "Got a problem? Get a boundary. It's *the* thing that's missing in your relationships." Like some advertisement for instant friendship success: "Are things getting weird? Then get some boundaries, and it will be all better."

I won't disagree, boundaries *are* life changing, friendship reviving, but I also think they are wildly oversimplified and misapplied far more often than not. In fact, in many ways, setting boundaries in friendships is far more difficult and time consuming than just breaking things off and walking away. By like, a lot. But why, you ask?

Let's break it down.

You've got two people. The boundary maker and the boundary receiver. In well-developed friendships, it moves back and forth, like a dance, with each person taking their steps in time.

Think back to a moment when you were on one side of a boundary. How did it feel to receive? If you were the one setting the boundary, how did it feel to express? What did you need to change if you were the one setting the boundary? If you were the one receiving it, did it feel like clarification was okay to ask for?

Once I bought a blouse from a friend of a friend, and I stopped by her house to pick it up. She said she wouldn't be home when I came by and I could just try it on at the door. I was fine with making sure no weird neighbors were nearby while I quickly tried on the top to make sure it fit. But when I got there, I heard kiddos playing, and I thought, *Oh, she is home, maybe she thought I was coming at a different time, I'll just knock to see if I can try it on with a mirror in a bathroom instead of in her front yard.*

Her husband answered the door, and their kids were playing. I explained that I was buying this top from her and he said it was fine if I came inside and tried it on. I went to their guest bathroom, shut the door, quickly tried on the two blouses she had for me, decided to take one and leave the other. Then, I left. Easy-peasy, as they say.

A week later I got a phone call.

Apparently, I wasn't supposed to knock on the door, and her husband shouldn't have let me in. They had a spoken boundary, and I was politely informed that I had violated it. "No opposite sex in the house when the spouse isn't home." Awkward.

At the time, I felt bad. Then I was confused.

And then I was more than a little pissed off.

Her boundary wasn't my problem, and she never communicated otherwise. She said, "No one will be home." She could have said, "Someone will be home, but my house is not available for you to come in, so please don't knock." With that, I would have been like, "Got it, thanks!" Instead I went there under the impression that everyone would be gone and naturally thought there was a mix-up. Her husband could have also just said, "Sorry, you can't come in, house rules." I would have been like, "No worries, sorry to bother you." Instead, I got a talking to weeks later about how I didn't respect an invisible boundary that wasn't my responsibility to abide by or know.

This example is why I get annoyed when people throw the boundary word around. I've had one too many friends take advantage of my relaxed and overly apologetic nature when they decide I've "overstepped" a boundary that's never been communicated but then switch gears when it's their turn to be on the receiving end. People *love* to be the ones setting boundaries, but they do *not* love being the ones who hear they've missed someone else's boundary.

The deal with boundaries is that we always want to have the power to set them, while simultaneously never being the person who "needs" a boundary set with them. As if we're only a lovable person if people don't have to set boundaries with us because we can perform in every relational circumstance so well it's as if we're the prima donna at the ballet. Which when you think about it, is silly, unless we're supposed to have this mind-reading power that no one has told me about? Oh wait, that's our hypervigilant trauma response, which is no way to have a friendship, but c'est la vie.

AN INVISIBLE SENSE OF OBLIGATION

For a very long time, as a friend, I had no boundaries. *People loved that.* It's like they could smell this invisible sense of obligation from a mile away and knew I thought it was my job in the friendship to always pay for dinner, gas, coffee, book the Airbnb (or the rental car), decide where we eat, know what to say and when to say it, ask the right questions, listen to the story, be the one who's more difficult and therefore the one that *obviously* needs to apologize. I was always watchful, the "paying attention" friend. The one who "didn't have her shit together" but also got the check. Why? It's what you have to be to fulfill the dream of the "good" friend. Someone who gives us everything we need without ever asking, or confronting, us for anything in return. We might not like hearing it said that way, but it's true. Even Yung Pueblo's list of traits describing a good friend is an impossible achievement.[2] It is beautiful to read, lovely to have, hard to find, and even harder to be.

This kind of performing in friendship reminds me of the perpetual winter without Christmas from *The Chronicles of Narnia*.[3] At least winter has Christmas, something to break the monotony of survival in the never-ending cold and dark. Winter without Christmas, or any Solstice celebration or other disruption to this often-difficult season, is like living a life full of connection with people who always expect something of you but never give anything in return. This happens far more often than we want to admit. Who hasn't weathered seasons, or years, where the people around you *don't* accept your limitations (a.k.a. boundaries) and don't make any effort to reciprocate the level of care you've offered them? For you, it's winter; for them, it's Christmas. That's the deal.

This is where we wade into the details, and the shame that shows up, when it comes to boundaries. When we have lived in a way that upholds someone else's lack of reciprocity masked as their good boundaries, we start to feel icky, confused, nauseous, and a little pissed off because the friend we've been is more like an assistant for someone we love, except we're not getting paid.

FAKE FRIENDSHIP

When people close to us repeatedly infringe on our boundaries in these subtle ways, we wake up to find ourselves in this kind-of-fake friendship. I say "kind-of-fake" because we can mistakenly think it means that (a) perhaps they don't know us that well, or (b) someone infringing on our limits would feel obvious to us from the beginning, and it's just about when we finally get uncomfortable enough to "deal with it."

Unfortunately, both of these ideas are untrue and perpetuate a false ideology around boundary crossing and boundary making that keep us in cycles of rejecting others or being rejected rather than allowing the discovery and communication of our limits to invite both people in the friendship to grow.

To the first, we assume that someone crossing our boundaries must mean they do not know us well. At the least, they're oblivious to the subtle cues we feel we've been giving. This serves in creating a power dynamic we may need to feel in order to set the boundary. (If they are not taking the hints, then we feel more "socially competent.") However, that misses and actually denies the fact that someone has found access to us around our borders, albeit often subconsciously. Obviously, a conscious violation of boundaries would be a moral problem and an offense against us. The situation most often is this friend actually knows us quite well and subconsciously has mapped our weak points as well as how to navigate around them[4] in order to experience what they believe they need, and perhaps feel they can only get, from us.

Which leads us to the second misconception.

When we think having our boundaries crossed feels disruptive, or that we've been "putting up with it" until we decide not to, we are being naïve. The reality is, because there's been connection, bypassing our own limits often feels *good*. Until it doesn't.

To understand this, we need to look at ourselves in parts. The next time you are talking with someone about a situation they are in, listen for when they say, "Well, part of me feels this. But another part of me feels that." If you've ever heard someone say these words, they are referring (consciously or not) to "parts" of themselves. There's a beautifully healing and evidence-based therapeutic methodology that was developed by Richard Schwartz precisely because he heard one of his patients use these kinds of phrases and decided to explore the idea that we, as Walt Whitman says, "contain multitudes."[5]

This way of knowing ourselves can also help us understand why our need for boundaries often feels so urgent. Essentially, a part of us has been enjoying the friendship without the limitations suddenly being expressed by another part that has arrived on the scene once our buttons have been pushed one too many times. But why isn't it obvious to us when our boundaries are being crossed?

We long to be subconsciously understood, for someone to see us and what we can offer, who we are, what we can give—which is part of our potential by the way. We desire this so deeply that we will show up for someone who acknowledges this about us, *even if* that understanding of who we are means someone oversteps our boundaries. The truth is that our friends (and don't forget—*we* are friends!) often do this in ways that activate the empathic, resourceful, and caregiving parts of who we are, and those parts of us love to be seen. The difference is, these parts of us aren't usually the same parts of us that know how to regulate and determine when and where to give our limited energy. The caregiving parts of us just want to do their job, which is to give.

Think of me, renting the car and figuring out all the travel details for my friends in the last chapter, or even Alyssa who probably heard her mom say she "felt bad" for me. We think of these kinds of traits as really tender, nurturing things—and they are. They are also quite powerful, and love to be given the authority in a friendship to care for and love another. When we have a friend overstepping those or other limitations within ourselves, especially when those parts of us haven't been valued or seen by others, getting to be the selfless friend feels like a cool drink of water. We are providing for someone the Christmas they've never had, that we've never gotten, and at least someone doesn't have to survive an endless winter as long as we are in their lives!

This is something we don't talk about: how good it feels to blend our limits with our love for a friend. There are places in us that want to lose our identity in another, to know so well what it's like to walk in their shoes that we forget we have a pair of our own.

THE NEW WILD WEST MAIN STREET SHOOT-OUT

The lack of mutual ownership in friendship in setting boundaries, or in communicating that our boundaries have been crossed, is due to the fact that we're invested on either side prior to any boundary being set. It is equally strategic for the person letting their boundaries be overstepped so they have the power of giving in a friendship as it is for the person getting the benefit of being cared for. Asking for mutuality will change the relationship in ways neither one of us are prepared for if that has been a theme in our past friendship dynamics, like a delicately balanced economic connection.

If we've found a way around the limitations of another, it is a part of what makes the friendship feel "special," that we have something they don't normally give or we've never gotten before. That feels good, and we feel good for figuring it out.

If we've found a limit that feels crossed by another, we usually aren't looking for how we've participated in creating that precedent and what we got out of it in the process. There's a kind of personal development superiority that exists right now when it comes to talking about boundaries. Like the new Wild West Main Street shootout. Whoever is aware of their limits and sets them first is the more evolved, the more healthy, the more self-aware one, and in this current social climate, you'd better not be slow to the draw.

I once had a friend I had a conflict with tell me, they "weren't ready to reconnect yet" on a voice memo. Based on what had happened between us, that felt fair enough, but it took me a minute to realize that what had also happened in that simple phrase was a shifting of blame in my direction resulting in a loss of agency for me. I had a different need, limitation, and boundary, which was that—reconnection aside—I needed clear communication and some closure in a reasonable amount of time. It felt odd to realize her boundary actually overstepped mine. Something like this is a perfect example of how we wield boundaries like weapons over other people's needs so that it remains a matter of "who said it first." No wonder we feel urgent when we realize a boundary needs to be set!

Even more tenderly, if the only way we received love when we were young (or what felt like it) was for us to live outside our comfort zone, we unconsciously think that's the only way for us to have connection. It's the price we need to pay in order for someone to see we have something of value to offer.

If you start to pay attention to the connection between your desires for and in friendship, and what you're doing to make that a reality, chances are there's more than a few ways you're filling in the gap between you and another person you love in hopes of keeping the relationship alive. Right now we're seeing it on social media through listed traits of a "good" friend or how to work on being a "better" friend. There's always someone who will overstep their limits to have connection and if it's not you, you could be the one left out. For example, if you're always the one buying dinner and can't ask for a split check, you might be forced to realize that maybe they don't want to hang out with you and they're just too smart to turn down dinner. Or you start to notice you're always the one inviting people to things that they gladly participate in, but then you realize you're not included in whatever they plan. It's as if there's this whole unwritten rule book of who has to give everything, who gets to ask for everything, and who gets connection as a result.

Pay attention to those details, the places where you found a way through someone's walls, or you outdid yourself. They are markers of who we are and what we have suffered to not be alone, the tells we have in our bluff for love. The place where we keep giving our chips away just so we don't have to realize no one wants to play with us.

I'm no stranger to loneliness, but one of the times I felt the most lonely was when I was a twenty-two-year-old with two kids under two.

THE (MESSY) BLUE HOUSE WITH A YELLOW DOOR

We bought our first house just after the 2008 crash and painted it blue with a yellow door. For a while, before we could afford to replace the porch, we had a plywood slat with two-by-fours as a ramp up to the front, not unlike a chicken coop. In addition to having two little kids under the age of two, I was expected to volunteer at church. My youngest daughter and I had major health issues, my partner ran two businesses, and I was starting to feel like I was going to lose my mind. I just couldn't keep up.

Looking back, it breaks my heart. That's too much for any human to manage alone. But that particular environment was one of abuse from a religious community, which meant my failure to perform in any one of the roles I'd been given was a fault of character and thereby a violation of others.

All this aside, we made a good decision and hired someone to come once a week who could help calm the madness and give me a break. They were there for four hours a week, and you'd think I would be resting with that time, but instead, I used it to get groceries. Yet during that blissful half-day, my house was clean and my kids were taken care of and I could be by myself for once.

This person saw the "me" behind the scenes. (Not that I've ever been good at pretending or wanting to be someone I wasn't.) They saw my house at its messiest, they saw me at my worst—in tears on the regular. They knew who I was in one of the most vulnerable seasons of my life. Having help brought enormous relief to me, and as part of our working relationship, they lent a listening ear.

When they transitioned out of that role and later got married, I naturally hoped our friendship would be something that would continue past the employer–employee relationship. Although

I recognized the care and level of vulnerability were very one-sided. (I received the care, was paying them, and they had access to a vulnerability about my life and home that no one else saw.)

What happened instead was that neither of us could stand the other. I felt a shift, that suddenly they were in this persona they stepped into as being "better" than me. Their house was cleaner, cuter, more organized, and their relationship with me changed from one of connection to condescension. All of this happened in subtle, unspoken ways, making it even more upsetting to me because I couldn't just "call it out." I wondered if I was jealous of them. If their life really was as good as they said it was . . . then maybe I was a failure at mine and they knew it from cleaning my house all those weeks. Having been so vulnerable with them, I felt blindsided by the transition and responded by being annoyed and suspicious. I didn't believe anything they said in any interaction we had, and I wasn't shy about saying so behind their back.

I was clearly resentful of what I felt to be (and it turned out later that it was) a portrayal of perfection they knew I had never lived up to. Because they had been the one to clean my house.

WHERE WOMEN TURN AGAINST EACH OTHER

More importantly, where we see women turning against each other is evidence of an environment that has set them up to do so—leading them to believe their survival or worth depends on it. At this moment in time, my friend and I were in such a place.

Then, their perfect life was disrupted by a traumatic event. I felt the much-needed guilt of how my actions toward them were harmful, and I decided to own up to the two-faced person *I'd* actually been while simultaneously accusing them of the same thing. After the dust had settled in their world, I asked if I could stop by and drove over to their house with the kind of coffee they liked in hand as a peace offering and delivered an apology without excuses or explanations. I simply said I was sorry. I had been mean, more than a bit jealous, and fake to their face. The clarity felt important to own up to, even though we already both knew how I had been acting. I didn't fall apart into tears, and I was genuinely remorseful. I have compassion on the frustration I felt at the change in my connection with them from safety to feeling my vulnerability used against me, and I still wish I hadn't been an asshole.

Nothing much happened after that, and I was okay with it. It was a relief to be honest and to also no longer be participating in the toxicity of taking other women down. The world we live in does enough of that already.

A year or so later, another shift happened for us, while I was in the midst of some other friend breakups. This new change was honestly delightful. The appropriate but risky truth-telling on my part opened the door for us to be frank with one another about more things we felt and needed to say about our relationship, and in doing so, we developed a mutual respect we then tested out with a slow-growing friendship.

MIRACLE-GRO FOR CONNECTION

Being specific and clear about the hidden ways we had harmed one another was like Miracle-Gro for connection. There is strength in that level of mutuality and goodness, in that kind of honesty as reciprocity. It wasn't even that we had harmed each other in the "same" ways. It was the fact that the things we had carried and known without knowing about how we judged or felt judged by one another were brought to the surface and cast aside. Through this exchange, we began to believe each other, to believe the other's experience and honor their perspective. What's more, this change in our relationship happened at a tumultuous moment in both of our lives.

On a hot July day, we found ourselves sharing these things with each other while running errands for an event. I was six months pregnant and (foolishly) overstepping my boundaries by coordinating this soirée, still trying to prove my worthiness to a community I didn't even feel safe enough in to have a messy house. As such things go, there was far too much to be accomplished in the amount of time left, but we carried on ticking off the tiny items of an endless to-do list. We were determined to get it all done. We walked and walked and made progress, drove some more, and it wasn't until 5 p.m. that we suddenly realized we hadn't eaten all day. By the time I finally sat down with a glass of water in Chipotle, I also realized I had not had anything to drink and started to notice the wear of the day's work on my body. My belly began to tighten and relax in that all-too-familiar way, these were not Braxton Hicks. I was exhausted and in denial, I was also in shock and panic. There was no way this could be labor. But as I sat there and told my body to calm down, it wouldn't. The contractions kept coming, regularly and closer together. I tried to stand up and started seeing spots. I had ignored my needs, and the effects of the heat, dehydration, stress, and fatigue were setting in.

I called my midwife, and she said my friend needed to drive me to the ER. My friend did and held my hand and counted and helped me breathe. Funny story is, when a crisis had happened in their life, to my shame, I had written it off as yet another thing I didn't want to believe. Now, here I was, in equally vulnerable shoes, asking for help. I wept on the whole way to the hospital saying, "I'm so sorry, I'm so sorry." It was humbling and heartbreaking in a way that changed me.

The story ends well. The nurse got an IV in me, and although the contractions stayed for several hours as I waited, terrified for what was going to happen next, eventually things slowed down and an ultrasound told me everything was fine (P.S. it was a girl), and that was that.

As the years passed after this moment, the bonds of our friendship continued to be sweet, tender, authentic, and strong. We didn't need it to be unshakable because we'd already been shaken. We didn't need to pretend because we'd already done that. I did feel I had found "the one." This was a level of connection I had never had.

SWEET TEMPTATIONS

It's important that you have a sense for how truly *good* this friendship was. Because if you're reading this, you've probably been through some friend breakups and there's probably a part of you that's also looking for that secret recipe or magical spark that can make for the kind of friendship you're longing for; the Disney-esque fantasy that somewhere out there is our BFF and kindred spirit, we just have to find them. In some ways, that part of us never stops looking, or more often, listening for the cues where we feel seen enough to trust and let someone in, or vice versa.

It's something all our senses are on the lookout for. For example, have you ever paid attention to the phrases you hear? The ones that reach a part of your soul like an iced latte on a summer afternoon. They're so close and maybe even exactly what you need, but not necessarily something you were looking for. You just know that when you hear it, it feels like you're home.

This is what my therapist surprisingly referred to as "temptations" one day in a session—temptations in friendship, to be specific. These are the little things someone says to us and we let them sneak past our boundaries because it feels so good to be seen.

If you have a religious background, you're probably thinking that's a weird use of this word—and you don't like it, but hear me out. What are the things you wish someone would say to you? They are usually things we know to be true about ourselves, but no one seems to acknowledge or notice.

Few things have been sweeter to me than someone saying, "I couldn't have made it without you" or "You're the only one I can tell this to." After being told I was a clueless friend, while making an effort for others to be seen or to have a good time, when I hear things like this, it means I've done not only what I'm "supposed to" but what I long for people to feel from me. It's like being labeled the opposite thing of whatever we are afraid of being called. If you're afraid you're bad, it's hearing someone say you're good; if you're afraid you're too much, it's hearing someone thank you for your vulnerability. It is intoxicating.

In this friendship, where we began with cordiality that turned to contempt and then to authentic connection, it made it easy for words like this to reach in and soothe more and more within us.

We both took a risk to give and a risk to receive, like them driving me to the hospital, or me apologizing at their house.

WE ALREADY KNOW HOW TO RECEIVE

We talk a lot about women and learning to receive. It's a poster-child type "problem," that women say they are "working on." This has always felt backward to me, because when we don't receive something it's usually because we don't feel safe and there's no harm in that, although it is worthy of being tended to. We treat women like their intuition is off and tell them they should be letting their guard down instead of looking at how people offering something might be the issue, because it is safer to give than to receive. Gifts, be they time, money, energy, and the excess to bestow them have been a long-standing form of social power. This is not to say that giving can't be vulnerable, but receiving is far more so. If you believe someone when they give you a compliment you are allowing yourself to be enjoyed, and that opens you up to being seen. If you receive someone's help, you are letting someone witness and engage your need for help. Giving is a role of power and authority, and receiving is deeply vulnerable.[6] Who of us hasn't had something we let ourselves accept from someone be turned against us or held over our head at some point in our lives? When it comes to friendship, if you generally find yourself on the initiating end of connection (and likely afraid of receiving), when somebody tells you words that resonate with everything your life is meant to bring, there is such sweetness, and you can't help but lean in.

Here are a few more of those "temptation" type phrases I heard from them in response to how I showed up for in our friendship:

"I want a relationship like yours."

"If there's anyone who could make that happen, it would be you."

"I couldn't have made it through this without you."

"Hearing your story gave me the ability to . . ."

These words felt like everything I longed to offer, and to hear them from my friend felt like being seen, which I was. In response, I found myself desiring to show up more and to offer more, because here was a place where someone wanted what I had to give, and it brought them closer to themselves, and it felt so good to me to be there.

The tricky thing about these "temptations" is that they are the phrases that blur our boundaries. They make us blend with the person who is speaking, and we feel we have fallen into a one-ness with them. If you're a human, there's a place within us where that desire for one-ness calls to something we will always long for.

When someone says, "You're a good mom, friend, person, etc.," their gratitude in the experience of knowing us relieves us too. We have permission to believe we are good and have performed well. Not out of a fear we'll disappoint, but because now, we get to be vulnerable. The affirmations we're afraid to desire most have been given to us and we melt. The part of us that cares so deeply for those we love and wants people to know how much they are worthy of being cared for feels like it has done its job when we hear those words. When someone sees this about us, the validation connects us to them in a way we cannot resist, because that caring part that also desires to be seen, is seen by them.

Like I shared in the beginning of this chapter, for the most part, I found ways to avoid receiving these things to keep from being vulnerable. If we are the "paying attention" friend, we will tell the people around us how amazing they are all. day. long. That way we don't have to attach to them through anything but our own terms because it is safer to give. Often, we will praise, care for, empathize with, but at some point, decide when the person we're giving to has asked for too much because we weren't actually paying attention to what we were getting out of watching them receive what we had to offer.

10,000 HOURS

Consider for a moment how we measure what it means to be an expert. Typically we evaluate it by longevity: How long have you been studying? In this relationship? Succeeding in your field? We measure this for all sorts of things: health, wealth, marriage, and career are some examples. They say it takes ten thousand hours to be an expert. People dedicate that kind of time to a lot of things in the world, and you can be good at so many things, it might not even be something that brings you success; it simply brings you joy, or it may even be something that isn't beneficial to you.

So when it comes to being good at giving like this, consider, if you spend three hours a day ignoring your heart, your body, your needs, and creating a construct where the basis for your world is self-denial while simultaneously affirming others, for years of your life, what you have actually become good at is not really caring for others, but rather ignoring yourself. However, because your focus is on the other and you have become very good at it, when they express gratitude for the care you've given them using the words you're longing to hear, it keeps you in a loop of ignoring yourself that is very hard to get out of. It's a cycle we often don't realize we are in. While it is good to care for others and feels good to do so, we fail to see that by knowing we can be a really, really good friend to everyone, we are missing ourselves. We miss the one person we are forced to live with and can't break up with no matter what we do, because it's us.

In all our calls for good friendship, we forget that befriending ourselves needs to be included. Honoring our worth, our needs, our desires just as much as we do our friends'. Everything is just an act if we don't. It's a different way of being on the stage, where we invite others to the front row seat of a standing ovation friendship performance. This is something we can only achieve if we leave behind whole parts of who we are, the honest parts of us that need us to listen to when we actually can't be good enough for the person in front of us. Because being a good friend has essentially meant being a selfless friend, and it's time we noticed how far that's asked us to move away from our own hearts.

WHAT DO YOU WANT PEOPLE TO SAY AT YOUR FUNERAL?

Missing ourselves this way is like living our life by answering the question of: "What do you want people to say at your funeral?" What do you care? You're dead. That entire question is oriented around the same idea of ignoring our needs and desires so that we can be what some external standard decides is "good," whether that's our partners, parents, lovers, or friends.

Think how exposing it would be to ask, "How do you want to feel on your deathbed, how do you want people to be *with you* in those moments?" instead of "What do you want people to say at your funeral?" You'd probably say you'd want to be seen and for them to allow the same with you. Why, then, do we work so hard to hide from being seen—which is to hide from having a self? Because having a self, knowing that self, and relating from that place is seen as selfish. But the truth is, our self is the core of who we are, and it is distinct, separate, and belonging solely to us, not to anyone else.

When we hide behind the idea of being "good," a.k.a. selfless, we are left deeply unknown. That's not to say what we bring others is inauthentic or manipulative. It's splitting hairs to isolate which part is the sweetness of your love or the seeking of another to confirm that your love is good enough. While our love and desire to be loved work well together in friendship, we often forget that those aspects of who we are also belong to just us. Most of how we have been raised and conditioned in society, is that who we are and what we want must be for, or completed by, someone else. We may think we have shed this ideology, until we find ourselves in some moment or season, truly alone, and the person in the mirror is unrecognizable without someone else to care for or to tell us we are doing a good job at it.

What this means when it comes to friendship and what we want out of it is that while we can share our desires by being, talking, and enjoying things together, at the end of the day, what we want in friendship belongs solely to us, and our friends' to them. Which is an oddly lonely place to be.

In our deep desire to be good, many of the ways we learned to relate to each other made our desires for friendship mold to a shape that isn't truly reflective of us and the connection we want. We are told to look for friendship without having been with ourselves first.

Why? Because it is a terrifying thing for our presence to actually matter—not as much to the other but to our own self. In fact, it's easier to express that in friendship than it is to honor the limitations or longings that live within us, on behalf of us.

Consider this: When we see the scars in others, we're ready with tender words to fill them in, and when we see a failure with ourselves, we're ready to own up and change. We jump to saying "I'm sorry" for transgressing a boundary or not reading between the lines. We are desperate in hidden ways to get away from the very things that make us who we are. Missing the beautiful truth that our flaws, wounds, failures, and mistakes belong to equally precious parts of us as all the beautiful, good, shiny traits that we want other people to see.

The way we relate to these parts of ourselves as well as our awareness and understanding of our own needs is a mixture of what we had and didn't have growing up. In being a good but not a selfish friend, we are seeking to offer the unconditional love we knew in part or did not know at all as children. We are trying to rewrite history with our friendships in our adult lives. Essentially this is mothering, which is a significant part of how we love the person next to us and how we show up intimately in friendship. Many friendships have an aspect of nurturing each other. What we might not know is that depending on our relationship with our own mothers, we typically reflect the emotions of a friend without wrestling with where our experience matters first. This is the result of attachment wounds.

AN INCREDIBLY BRIEF OVERVIEW OF ATTACHMENT[7]

Attachment theory is complex, and there are books and books written about it and its impact on our brains, bodies, and lives. It is a tender, and often very triggering thing to begin to learn about and to name for ourselves. The reason for this is because it was a time when we were truly without power over our circumstances. Whether as a tiny baby, energetic toddler, curious school kid, or angsty teen, how the people in charge of caring for us showed up, or didn't, creates a ripple effect into nearly every area of our lives today. The good news is our brains and bodies have the capacity to heal. So even if we grew up with "insecure attachment," we can mend these places in us to be able to attach securely with others as adults.[8]

However, just like friendship got handed the job of writing a happily-ever-after love story, we're also holding the failure of our parents as we look to connect with our peers in adult life. In order to understand this invisible burden on friendship, we first need to explore what it means to talk about how we "attached." While we treat things like boundaries as the hot topic to discuss around relationships, we cannot even begin to engage how to set them or how they impact us without a basic understanding of these childhood wounds.

There are three core parts to what makes up attachment and three *main insecure* attachment styles. I say *main* because there are delineations, and even as the field of psychology grows and research continues, these definitions are evolving to help us understand more of what is needed to heal.

The three core aspects of attachment are: attunement, containment, and rupture and repair. I love the work of Abby Wong-Heffter, and her definition of these concepts has stuck with me. She explains them like this:

Attunement is essentially someone looking at us: "I see your face, I reflect what you are feeling, you make sense and I understand you." Imagine you are a small child who has been crying and come to your mother. Imagine her placing her hands on your face and kneeling down at your level. Her face is showing you your own face in a way that lets you know what you are feeling matters and is real and that you are not alone. That is attunement.

Containment is someone who is looking at us but not escalating with us. They are saying, "Your feelings are yours, you belong to you, there is space between us and that offers you the safety of knowing you do not have to be something for me because I belong to me." Imagine you are still that small child who has run up to their mother, and she is looking at you and attuning to you, but she is also not becoming anxious or worried about how you feel; she is trustworthy because she has a boundary of her own feelings that makes space for you as the child to feel what you need. She lets go of your face at the exact moment you're ready and reminds you that, you too, belong to you and not to whatever just brought on these big feelings. You take a deep breath and turn back around to go play. That is containment.

Rupture and repair is the third element, and it is also the most painful one. I have heard it described as the unicorn piece of attachment, because it is so rare for us to have experienced it. We need all three components of attachment to be there for us to attach securely to our parents, including this one; however (and to young parents reading this, here's some good news), we only have to get things right 30 percent of the time in order for our child to securely attach[9] and repair is the key element in maintaining that. Rupture and repair is the caregiver responding, *in real time* (not days, months, or sometimes years later) to say, "I messed up, this is on me, I should not have done that. You do not have to forgive me or make me feel better. I just want you to know I am responsible for what happened and how I hurt you, and I'm sorry. And if you need to hear more from me about how I hurt you or would like to share more with me about how you feel, I am here to listen." That is repair.[10]

Honestly, I had to stop writing in the coffee shop where I am right now and put my head in my hands for a good twenty minutes before finishing that paragraph. Most of us are starved for repair, and what that means for ourselves and not just our friendship is that we really don't hold much hope for anything to be resolved, or for anyone to own up when they've hurt us, or for us to even be forgiven if we messed up, especially for those of us who never got the repair we needed and deserved from our parents.

The three main types of insecure attachment (not including secure, which is where we got attunement, containment, and repair) are anxious, avoidant, and disorganized. Again, attachment theory is deeply complex and intricate, and these are incredibly brief overviews. Allow me to describe them continuing to use the example of our faces:

When we have anxious attachment, we have had a loss of attunement and had to be approved of by others in order to be allowed to feel containment. Anxious attachment is like always looking for a face to reflect who you are and what you feel because you are not allowed to know yourself, or if you do, that means you have done something wrong because you did not attune to your caregiver. If you decided anything for yourself about how you felt, that meant you would be punished, so you stay in a constant state of unknown about who you are in order to stay safe.

Avoidant attachment is like moving away from all the faces because you can only rely on yourself, and if you ask for anything from anyone else, you know you're going to be misunderstood at the least, ignored at best, or harmed at worst. You've done something wrong if you show what you need and you ask too much of your caregiver. You have to know and figure yourself out, otherwise you will be punished, and as a result, the ache of your needs is buried deep inside.

Like I said, it is painful stuff.

Disorganized, this overview's final insecure attachment style, *may*[11] indicate significant childhood trauma. This can be from thousands of cruel subtleties or big recurring harm. It is in many ways a combination of anxious and avoidant but entirely dependent from second to second. You can trust no one's face, but you also know your survival will depend on if and when you do. Because of what you have suffered, relationships are like being in a labyrinth where you never know what is around the corner. While you have become very good at survival, every new encounter with someone, even if they are kind, feels like the setup of surviving the nightmarish world of your childhood. While every person with insecure attachment deserves the safety of therapeutic care to heal, it is especially important for you to know that what happened to you is not your fault and you can heal. You are worthy of relationships and friendships where your heart is able to take all the time you need to settle and feel safe in being seen and eventually cared for. In addition, you hold insight and awareness beyond what most understand and deserve to be honored for all that you bring to connection.

Moving on from this intense and brief overview of attachment, let us return to what this means for our friendships and the things that people say to us (often that we wish our mother had said). When we, or our friend, feel cared for and say so, if we did not securely attach, it is very easy for those "temptations" to begin a cycle of re-enactment in a friendship because we are trying to rewrite the story of us with our caregivers. Once that's set in motion and feeling good to give and receive in, it is very difficult to stop because that would mean attuning to the loss that lives in very young stories.

Alice Miller in her book, *The Drama of the Gifted Child*, talks about how secure attachment in childhood is the place we experience unconditional love for ourselves, from our caregivers, and if we did not get it then, we never will.[12] It's a harsh truth, but she's right. You may feel like you cannot breathe reading that, especially after hearing about the things you should have received from your parents. It is such a painful reality, like moving from the comfort of our mother's womb into a cold world yet again, but this time it is as adults learning that it is not our job, nor is it our friends', for us to love one another unconditionally. Love from a parent to a child is meant to be unconditional, which then facilitates the development of that child into becoming an adult who understands the value and boundaries of themselves. Securely attached children grow up to be humans who know what it means to value and hold both the experience of themselves and the other in relationships without getting mixed up in the process.[13]

It is a tough thing to name or believe there was any failure or loss in our childhood. Our instinct is to protect our parents at all costs, to use our ability to understand circumstances to protect us from the ways we were harmed, which ultimately protects us from owning our experience. Consider this: we will protect our parents until we allow them to be human. And we will protect our parents to the detriment of our friends.

Here's how this ends up working out in our friendships. We look for a way to right the wrongs in our own stories, or be better than people who failed us, and—usually unconsciously—find a way to make up for what we have not even recognized we've lost.

But here's the beautiful and funny thing: when we begin to know ourselves and our stories (the things we have lost that we can never get back), it frees us up to connect with what we actually want in friendship—and even life. We have been handed this false idea that "good" friendship is something fulfilling, except . . . (and this is a bit of philosophy here for you) we cannot *share* the things we desire, or more importantly love, because by its very nature, desire is something that can only be our own in order to exist. It is a longing for something that is always "not yet."[14] When we step into friendship connected with ourselves, we are stepping into a relationship that exists precisely because of something we cannot possess. We don't *have* friendships, we *experience* them together.

WE HAVE TO LOOK AT THE WHOLE STORY

In this chapter's friendship story, we had the pillars of attachment together—even rupture and repair! We had gone through life changes and self-changes and remained connected. Things felt secure. I believe most friendships where we take the risk to be vulnerable with each other feel secure to us. We also reflect that security back to each other with the same words that act like "temptations" to overstep our boundaries. And I say that to remind you that there isn't a formula or a right answer when it comes to the friendships we have or the friends we want to be. What's important is that we look at the whole story, without writing things off as good or bad, and that we include all of ourselves in the process.

After we had moved to different states and started to rebuild our individual lives, my friend and I stayed well connected for a while in truly good and life-changing ways, until things ended abruptly. To summarize my history before finishing this story, I was not raised by parents who accepted me. As such, I am very good at creating acceptance for people in my friendships. It's part of my still-healing insecure attachment that is both a gift in my ability to see people and a curse because I will neglect myself. I still find myself carrying the responsibility of this role and caught in the places with friends where I eventually wake up to what I need and what I shouldn't be holding for the other person. Which is where I found myself again in this friendship.

One of the things I loved about my friend is that they are what I would call a "tourist of experience." Their courage to try new things, or do something outside the norm, created a general sense of freedom. They were fun to be around and it made things like traveling together more enjoyable. Where I found myself caught was when the experiences of their life they had asked me to support began to conflict with each other. They had confided in me how their marriage was and that they wanted to fight for it, then with no warning, months later, told me they were sleeping with other people unbeknownst to their partner and expected me to be happy for them. I felt conflicted and confused—put in a position I did not want to be in. I also felt the pain of wanting my friend to know, while I was struggling with their decisions, I didn't think that meant they were doing anything other than finding a way to come alive, and that deserved to be honored. This is something all of us are on a path toward, in one way or another, and it's a path that is much easier if we don't have to walk it alone.

What I didn't acknowledge in myself about trying to stay in this space of showing my acceptance for them despite how I felt is that it was actually harmful. I was trying to give them unconditional love, the thing we can only get from our mothers.[15] I failed to see that making someone feel and know they are accepted by you is different from simply *being* accepting and allowing them to wrestle with their own inner knowing of that truth. In attempting to let our friendship shift again as their life and desires changed, I disregarded the fact that I was now in a space between them and their partner that I had not consented to, nor did I want to be a part of.

They had confided something to me about their life that I did not ask to know—simply because it felt private—and I wasn't given a choice before hearing the information. While I felt acceptance of what they were exploring about their sexuality (we'd both come from the background of purity culture), what they said also made me feel grief—mostly because I'd been made a secret keeper without being asked. And I suddenly (but silently) stopped playing the role of actively creating acceptance and spaciousness. Something their parents did not offer them, but that I had been.

The nuance of this was taking the risk that I would be, in some part, replicating their own trauma. By allowing my experience to matter (the grief and discomfort of keeping a secret), I knew I was no longer playing the role that brought me the things I had received: the tempting phrase of "You're the only one I can tell this to," and leaving them to be very alone in a very real way in a difficult time in their life. Something their parents had also done.

Unconnected to them and this encounter, I had finally been taking an honest look at my own desires, limitations, and experience of what was happening in my life and started allowing it to matter. And I had found exhaustion, I had found grief, I had found a desire to not be put in the middle of a conflict that wasn't mine to solve or mediate—even if maybe I could.

For my part, I felt the shift in me didn't need a direct conversation with them. I just engaged in different topics and parts of our friendship, things we still shared in common and enjoyed, because I believed we could evolve without that. We had evolved before. Maybe I was right in that naïve way, not evaluating and owning what I had received through the years through the giving and receiving of being a confidant in our friendship in other ways. I was, as it turned out, wrong, and things were near an end between us, despite my hopes.

Something I said to their partner at the time (as couples we were all friends) was taken out of context and used by that partner as something against my friend in a disagreement between them as a couple. It was a hot mess. This is the kind of space I had gotten myself into because of my desire to offer acceptance and show up well—while disconnected from myself. I discovered this exchange had happened when I sent a random text a few weeks later and received a long reply that was them breaking up with me by telling me I had betrayed them. While I disagreed with them at the time, in a way I had. Just not in the way they thought.

They had been so good to me. I received from this friend so many beautiful things. I also gave freely of goodness and beauty to them. We moved through some difficult transitions together while being miles apart. I am still so grateful for this friendship, but then I became a selfish friend. I felt my limit and saw the role I was playing and had to let go. Things I *never* wanted anyone to feel from me, things I *always* said I would be, roles I was committed to playing, needs of my own I was committed to ignoring. I did something I never thought I would do and stopped listening to the subtext of what they desired of me in friendship and stepped away. In retrospect, it might have been braver and more honoring for me to step into the vulnerability of having a conversation with them about this rather than keeping this change to myself. But that is how I showed up, and what I felt was best at the time.

THE TROUBLE OF KNOWING EXACTLY WHAT TO SAY

This was also the trouble because I actually did know exactly "what to say" to make things right. I knew how to be with them in the way that they wanted, and I didn't do it. I realized making things "right" meant compromising myself and the limits of what I was willing to offer when it came to continuing to hold this evolving space in a way that they felt held in our friendship by me. I didn't mind the "mess" they were making in their life, but I didn't want to spend my nervous system's energy on making space for that because I had my own experience to tend to.

So I chose myself, to be present as myself, and lost the friendship. In not betraying me, I did betray her.

The truth is, most of the time, we make the decision to stay connected with ourselves only after we realize we've been acting outside of integrity under the illusion of showing up for the other person (which is really a betrayal of them, the same way it is of ourselves). Part of the reason we will either stay in a friendship like this or cut people off and label them is because the presence of resentment in our friendships reveals the wounds of our attachment. And confronting those places within ourselves—as we've already seen in this chapter—is sometimes unspeakably painful.

Of course we want to celebrate authenticity, empathy, or integrity as qualities we love in others and have acknowledged in us. What we don't realize is that owning those things as real about what we desire and who we are will at some point involve betrayal.[16]

This may be confusing because we think of betrayal as the antithesis to friendship, with loyalty being the core. Here again is this desire we've been handed of who we ought to be to one another or what we should want when it comes to finding community, as we find ourselves. Anyone who tells you that this bind of betrayal to stay connected to yourself will suddenly no longer exist when you "find your people" is lying to you, and in fact, it will keep you and your friendships in subconscious cycles of fear of being left, rather than knowing the greatest gift you perhaps can give to one another is that you won't use your connection to stop either one from your own growth. Even if that means the betrayal of someone you love to stay connected to who you are. Or having the courage to walk away from a friendship because it invites your friend to move closer to themselves.

In *Women Who Run With the Wolves*, one of my favorite books on healing and self-discovery, Jungian psychoanalyst Clarissa Pinkola Estés writes of coming back to ourselves in this context:

> Some women are afraid that those around them will not understand their need for return. And not all may. But the woman must understand *this* herself: When a woman goes home according to her own cycles, others around her are given their own individuation work, their own vital issues to deal with. Her return to home allows others growth and development too.[17]

Without a sense of our own identity, we cannot be with someone who is claiming theirs. We will either detract from their development or lose ourselves in their new orbit. Neither of which serve either one of us (though one may "feel" better than the other as losing ourselves means leaning on the inner work of someone else).

To pull away may feel like rejection of the other and their new life, but in truth, we are acknowledging the space between us, a sacred and holy thing that more of us must learn to do in order to become more fully ourselves on behalf of one another.[18]

That's the interesting nature of betrayal when we risk our presence and owning ourselves in a way that's truly authentic. It's easier to tell ourselves we are just selfish, or to say that our friend is. It's less painful to claim we're just not accepted, rather than recognizing that may not be what we need or what they have to give. When we find ourselves in this conflict on either side in a friendship, we are at the crossroads of our desire for unconditional love. We will expect unconditional acceptance from our friends if we haven't received unconditional love from our parents. It is okay that we want this, that mothering love, with its unquestioning acceptance, an ever-expansive heart, and the hope of being heard no matter what it is we have to say or the implications of it. But when we look to the faces of our friends to fill this void in us, we miss the gift that is at the heart of friendship itself.

In the parent–child relationship, things are one way. The things a parent accepts and the way they love their child is not something the child should have to offer back. When we grow up, this experience of love from our parents is meant to shift; if things go well, we are nurtured into adulthood, and the relationship with our parents becomes peers. They are no longer our authority, nor are they our caregiver; we have learned to know and tend to ourselves because of their tender care. It is this two-way relationship that friendship invites us to experience. We meet one another, accepting of our own conditions (which is actually what makes space for freedom), and as long as we are still searching for the love we never got, we will miss the beauty that's found in the conditional love of the friendship that's right in front of us.

Instead of being the adults we are and learning to trust our friends, or not, as part of the uncertainty it is to live life together, we look for something unconditional that no longer exists. But that was never what friendships were supposed to do.

The things my friend told me about their new life, I felt in that moment, were not about seeking connection, they were about an acceptance no one could give them but themselves. And I chose to get out of the way by accepting myself where they could not. I accepted my confusion and inner turmoil; I did not play the part of a mother helping what should have been a teenager freely exploring their sexuality. The parts of me they had asked to invest in the desires for their marriage were overwhelmed by now being told that my support and loyalty of them meant switching directions to their new life and desires. Not to mention our partners were friends, and not to mention that my own relationship felt like it was on thin ice at the time—and I actually wanted to stay. I just couldn't do it, but even more true was that they didn't need me to—whether they knew that or not at the time. Obviously, I didn't have the emotional resources to "go with the flow," to carry a secret that they were sleeping with other people, and then go have a normal conversation with my partner where he was sharing how heartbroken he was for his friend.

When they confronted me with my betrayal, I realized that by not asking them to also accept me by being vulnerable about the conflict I felt, I had created an illusion of acceptance for them. I was protecting myself from a deep fear of rejection from my own attachment wounds by not allowing my experience to matter too. I knew our relationship to that point had been one of such sweet fulfillment and reflection that it was time to move into discovering what was really ours to give to each other. I wasn't sure what things would look like, but I knew things were going to change. I just assumed change could happen without me communicating how I felt. I responded to their secret of what they needed and wanted, by keeping myself and what I needed and wanted and felt, secret.

It's a complex thing to realize that not letting our experience matter in friendship with others might actually be what's more selfish, whether you choose to share your experience with them or not.

The loss of their friendship hurt, but less so than any others, I think, because I was certain of my love and presence and honoring of both theirs and my experience—realizing that knowing these details about myself and within myself was enough for me. Hoping that they would know the same could be true for them too. I hope, and believe, they do now.

But friendships don't usually end easily. Instead, they have a way of haunting us.

WHO WILL GUARD THE THINGS SPOKEN NOW?

A year or so later when I started building my business online, we hadn't communicated since the breakup text. Their new partner, someone I didn't even know, trolled me a few times. I would write something about authenticity and healing, and they would comment rude things from different accounts. I finally blocked them all, or they got tired of it and moved on.

Being attacked like that, even a year after the fact, returned me to the sorrow and genuine fear it was to lose a friend. The intimacy and honesty and presence that is shared makes it hard to believe it was once real when the friendship is over. Who will guard the things spoken between the two of you now? Will one person need to throw the other one under the bus in order to avoid the pain of loss?

This is the quest for the unconditional and forever showing itself again. That desire for loyalty may still be there, and if it is ours, it will always be there. The temptation is to say, "If something is good and real, then it will always be, and if it doesn't, then it really was never good at all." The ending of a story is hard to hold when it is not followed with a sequel with the same characters. It is hard to know what to believe was real.

I felt turned into a lesson when I read those snide internet comments engineered to make me question my integrity. What they chose to say, the fact that I didn't even know this person, the out-of-the-blue nature meant I had been watched and they had waited and read my work and as soon as I shared something personal about myself, they struck.

It is easy to characterize the friends we've lost; it also keeps us on a loop of looking for that one person to check all the boxes and for them to keep checking them. It makes us look for faults and problems and flaws where there might actually be none. Both people might actually be growing. This person left their partner and started seeing and living with other people. I was sad because the context I'd known them in, they had asked me to emotionally invest in them and a life they now no longer wanted, and while I had cared about those now-gone desires in them, I also honor and celebrate them in the courage of moving more toward themselves.

It's no secret that life and love bring changes, beyond what we could ever expect. What continues to haunt me though from this friendship and others is when I do the same, bringing a desire for what's been expected of me or who I am to change, I am rejected. Alongside the gift of conditional love that is found in friendship, is the vulnerability. There are those who will tell us we are no longer worthy of self-acceptance if we fail them. Many of us are in friendships that are still a one-way street.

This friendship was the start of my wondering if friends have the job of being there forever for each other so it's easier for our romances to end and begin again. Like a security deposit on still having shared history with someone, even if we find a new partner.

I still loved our friendship and connection, I always will—though now as a memory. We were both changing in some ways beyond our control. And in some ways my way to control what was happening and how I felt about it had been to take on a role of creating acceptance for them that wasn't actually mine to give.

Which was selfish but didn't look like it.

It only did when I let go.

CHAPTER SIX

HOW TO BE A TOXIC FRIEND

"Anything that's human is mentionable."

—Fred Rogers[1]

Friend breakups happen when we need our friends the most.

Friend breakups also happen when one person is honest and the other is not. When friend breakups happen, our ex-friends often tell other people the details of what happened. Or said another way: what we call toxic in other people or in past friendships is really just when we're finally speaking about what was in the room the whole time. It's just that now those conversations are not happening between the two friends who were involved.

A toxic friendship leads to the kind of breakup we all know happens but nobody wants to be caught talking about. As a result, the toxicity we feel when a story like this does get brought up is, in part, because we are having that conversation with somebody else instead of the person we hurt.

Those of us who pretend our choices were not a part of the problem find ways to absolve ourselves of the guilt by talking about our friends behind their back and calling it something else.

Those of us who feel our choices were somehow the entirety of the problem try to find ways to survive, because the abandonment of a friend on top of whatever we were experiencing in our lives creates a shame that is nearly unbearable to live with.

I remember thinking as a teenager that things would be different when we were all adults. Surely, we would be kinder as adult women. Surely, there would be less of a need for power plays, gossip, humiliation, or manipulation. As a lonely twenty-two-year-old mother of two, when I met Tracy, a mom in her late thirties who was fun, relatable, and didn't pretend to "have it all together," I thought I'd made it out of the woods of female pettiness. Having played the "adult" for most of my childhood, being friends with someone older than me and a little further along in life felt like such a relief. Plus, I felt she just liked me.

What most friendships that end hold in common is that they become about what happened to cause the breakup. All the sweet memories are discarded, erasing the identity of the friendship that was once enjoyed. We manage the heartbreak by making it into a lesson. We do things like turn everything that happened before the rift into missed "red flags," and soon enough any memory of shared goodness with one another is gone.

When we go through a messy breakup of any kind, it's only natural to find a reason. In fact, we might fear we'll go crazy if we don't. A lot of times we find that reason in the other person, like "We're just in different places," or in ourselves, "I wasn't in a good place," or in the circumstances, "It wasn't meant to be." The funny thing is, we use every one of these explanations in conversation with *another* person, typically a new or mutual friend, *about* the friendship we used to have. Whether we want to admit it or not, this liminal space of writing off somebody that we used to know is still a part of the friendship, a part of the loss—even though the two of you are not speaking anymore.

When we turn people into lessons, we all become less human, and our labeling of someone as toxic speaks to our fear of being the mess they found themselves in. We distance ourselves by explaining away why we were ever foolish enough to connect with them in the first place. This speaks a deep truth about the connection between our loneliness and sense of worthiness, illustrating how we live in a world where our ability to maintain a friendship regardless of what life throws at us is what equates to our integrity, emotional health, or enoughness. Basically, it ensures that we aren't toxic. There's a whole world when you read between the lines of the people you've left behind or how you were written off by somebody you once thought you could trust implicitly.

Welcome to the hidden life of failed relationships.

STRANGERS AND FICTION

This is the story of my friendship with Tracy. We had this funny running joke about our connection when we met—it was spontaneous, and it felt real. The fluidity of acceptance and relaxation of the beginning of our friendship reminded me of the way you feel on a seventy-two-degree day. It was just easy, fun. We both had a similar background in religion that we had, mostly, left. That ideology always had an agenda for friendship and community like it had to be oriented around very serious "godly" things. So connecting with her over just normal life stuff felt amazing. We could talk about the real and the hard things while laughing over drinks about something dumb the next minute. We traveled together, randomly had each other over for dinner, and watched each other's kids so the other one could get a break. There was a kind of reciprocity. It was a community. It was sweet and felt uncomplicated.

There was a movie she liked that she introduced me to called *Stranger Than Fiction*. She loved this narrative of a depressed author persuaded by a persistently optimistic main character who lived in the real world. Although the author writes him into disaster after disaster to break him down, one day he shows up at her house revealing that he is a real person. Having discovered he was a character in her book, he became determined to find her, hoping his desire and love of life would persuade her to stop writing tragedies for him. She tells him she has plans to kill him off, at which point he leaves her house and awaits his uncertain fate by living fully optimistically and joyfully in the world around him. The movie ends with him getting hit by a bus and waking up in a hospital with nearly every bone broken in his body and a smile on his face—living. The author resigns what others had said would be the novel of her career to an ending of serendipity and humor when, as told by her agent, it could have been the drama of the era.[2]

My friend loved this movie, and I loved her for it. Ever filled with a playful and amusing hopefulness, she seemed to have a refusal to see things for other than the bright side, although she knew I didn't share this perspective. I preferred to hold more to the melancholic philosophy of the author in the story. Terrible things did happen in life, and they needed to be talked about. In fact, they sometimes served to highlight what was good. But this wasn't something we needed to agree on.

This breakup, even as I sit writing in a coffee shop thousands of miles and years away, churns in my stomach with the americano and pastry. I don't wonder if I'm able to write the truth. It's not fear that grabs my mind back from this work of bringing to light certain details. It's the fact that there was love there. I felt seen and connected to her during a time in my life when I needed to be seen and connected. And rather than being the melancholic writer who has a vendetta for their annoyingly optimistic main character, part of healing is being honest about who people were to us even when things did not end well, or happily ever after.

The details of any friendship ending are difficult to talk about when we hold the goodness and harm of what happened. In fact, when I've risked being seen in this story by others, people back away. As a result, I lived for a long time believing that everything that happened was my fault. When in fact, none of it was. That's the thing about toxic friend breakups: the circumstances surrounding us leave us feeling entirely alone in them. Telling ourselves that if people knew the real story (like the friend calling us toxic did), we would be rejected again before ever getting a chance to prove that we are good, or that we've changed, or that what happened wasn't fair.

The lie of having to be the toxic friend is that you deserve to feel isolated and ashamed of who you are or what you're going through, and that no one will ever understand or accept you here. Which is why your friend who you thought you could trust has suddenly turned their back, only to talk about what happened with you to someone else.

The lie is that you are alone in this circumstance. The truth is, while you are alone in your unique circumstance, you are not alone in your felt experience.

This friend breakup was torturous, and my entire family was dragged through the mud in a small town with things going so far as to be made up about us in addition to none of our boundaries being respected. I could not believe someone I had confided in during the most vulnerable moments of my life would betray me like this.

This is why the unraveling of this particular friendship, out of all I share in this book, shook me to the core. There was so much play, so much delight, inside jokes, witty sarcasm, and a general willingness to just enjoy the moment. So, it wasn't a slow fade when things went bad. It was literally a nightmare that happened overnight.

At the exact time when I needed my friends the most, they were not there, and not only that but at the initiation of Tracy, they began talking about who I was based on the circumstances around me.

One of the inside jokes she and I enjoyed was a phrase we would use with each other to preface being honest. Whenever we had something awkward that happened or needed to be said, the words "full disclosure" were used to start. Not only was there play in this friendship, there was authenticity and a shared investment in open communication, or so it seemed. And like the clueless friend I was, I leaned into our connection with a lot of trust in her confidence and influence in my life.

She showed herself to be someone I could count on when things were difficult, showing up to hold space for me on more than one occasion. I confided in her on some of the hardest days of my life and shared some of the most vulnerable things that have ever happened to me, to which she listened so kindly and empathically; the kinds of things I was afraid would not be believed—that should never happen to anyone. I didn't have a therapist at the time, and I just implicitly trusted our connection and her commitment to keeping it in confidence.

In the days of the unraveling of our friendship, she told me she never believed me or the things I shared. She thought I had made these traumatic stories up, and when I confronted her about it, she told me she wasn't honest with me at the time because "that wasn't what *you* needed at that moment." My connection with Tracy had felt so good initially, and suddenly all the pieces of even tenderness and empathy I had thought were real in our friendship, were pulled out from under me.

One of the complex things about conflict in friendship is that we think it either shouldn't happen because we are friends or that we should be able to resolve it because we are friends. But conflict brings up so much more than what we are or have experienced in our friendship with someone to that point.

Conflict brings up past trauma. It highlights differences we might have pretended weren't there. It creates difficulty in a relationship where we're used to just having things be easy. A friendship is a place where we're supposed to be able to relax, vent, and be understood, right? So if you can't resolve or never have conflict, was it ever a friendship?

The reality is that if we can't have conflict in a friendship, we will lose the friendship.

A toxic friendship is one that can't metabolize conflict.

Let me tell you a story about something that's actually toxic.

KILZ PAINT AND CONFLICT

Think about a food you never liked as a kid but were forced to eat (for me, it's bananas). As an adult, you probably don't force yourself to eat that food. Or maybe you eat foods you don't like (for reasons I will never understand), but maybe you get tired of being the only one who does that or trying to convince others to "just try it."

Now think about the conflict you experienced while growing up (and I'm guessing it wasn't the good kind). It probably feels like having that food on your plate again or, worse, when it shows up in friendship today. It may even feel toxic, and this is where it gets interesting.

Do you know what actually makes something toxic?

The way it enters the body.

I learned this when my twenty-month-old kid dipped his pacifier in a tray of KILZ oil-based paint, and I called poison control terrified my child was going to die. They said he would be fine unless he had breathed it in while swallowing (in which case he might die). but otherwise he would be 100 percent fine.

He was fine.

End of story.

Who knew you could ingest something that's extremely toxic (which is worse than food we don't like) and not die . . . but what does that have to do with friendship? Well, sometimes conflict or the calm before that storm looks more like KILZ oil-based paint than just eating your vegetables as a kid. (Which, I won't lie, can be traumatic.)

We are afraid of conflict, because at some point somebody fed us paint and said it was food. We definitely didn't like it and it actually made us sick. It's no wonder we're afraid of, or angry at, people labeled *toxic*, except, that we all have toxic parts of us. Pretending toxic is only somebody we used to know is just perfectionism with a rebrand.

Toxic is a warning label on things that harm our bodies but serve a needed purpose that's helpful to our daily lives when used properly. I think the more we misuse this word about past friendships, the more afraid we become of the parts that connected with that person instead of healing the trauma of the friend breakup.

The definition of *toxic* is poison. There's a range in lethal quality for the word, and something by itself isn't toxic. It's how it enters the body, or in this case, the friendship.

Conflict is often fueled by the fear of the external circumstances that have happened to us as humans over the course of our lives. The painful thing is that we are bringing in our own stories to overlay meaning, intention, or impact that may not exist between us and the friend we're trying to resolve things with. The things that happen *to* us are not our fault; it's what we do next that matters.

As long as the conflict is something that doesn't have to do with the friendship or something happening that impacts one, or both, of you, it's easy to talk about with your friend. In fact, we do! Talking through conflicts or things that you're going through in your life is one of the gifts of friendship. We have someone "on our side" to process things with.

This is why conflict in friendship is hard to talk about! We simply aren't used to having that normalized as part of our connection because it's been the place we go when things aren't working out in our lives or with somebody else. And as long as that somebody isn't you or your friend, things will be fine.

The other tender thing about falling out in a friendship is that the confidentiality and privacy of your relationship gradually disappears. This is when things start to get messier than is "socially acceptable." Which is devastating, because it's something we've relied on as a part of building the friendship. When we confuse toxic circumstances with people, by talking about what someone is going through that we once protected that space with (even calling them toxic in an "anonymous" yet public way), we are actively harming someone.

NINETY DEGREES AT A TIME

We sat in a car in the cold, damp parking spot of a local open space. The rain fell, and she gave me a book and some sound advice. Stuff in my relationship was falling apart, and she had been through the same thing. And for once in my life, something had happened that someone had been through before, and I didn't feel alone. She held my hand over the console between us until I had to let go to nurse my six-week-old baby who started crying in the back seat. It was the beginning of the end of so many things, but neither of us could know that yet. I remember the shape of her hands and the rings she wore and the way she gestured with a cup of coffee while talking, making concentric circles on a napkin with the watermark from the mug. It spoke thoughtfulness, determination, and hopefulness for the ways she had found to hold reality with that positive spin that was so important to her to maintain. Rotate, set the mug down, rotate and set it again. Ninety degrees at a time.

That was the last time we talked in a way where our friendship still felt real and intact.

A few days later, I learned some things that disrupted my ability to trust or confide in her. I was at an impasse with information that made my safe friend suddenly unsafe. I was left in a bind of pretending I had never heard this information or telling her the next time she checked in on me exactly why I'd be vanishing from our friendship as we knew it. I chose the latter, hoping, blindly, that her eternal optimism would be like swallowing KILZ paint that would pass through us if only we didn't choke and breathe it in.

The sun was out, I texted her that I needed to come over and tell her something. And as I relayed the information outside my car, I began to wonder if she already knew. Because she didn't seem surprised. Sad, perhaps? But not surprised. I won't really ever know.

It was a situation where I didn't know what the heck to do. None of us do when these kinds of toxic circumstances hit us. We're basically left to figure them out on our own. Everything that was happening to me, on top of having a newborn, felt like drowning. I didn't know what to do and didn't pretend that I did. I took a risk with what I felt our friendship could handle, maybe not survive, but I thought there could be space for understanding since she had already dealt with the exact same thing in her relationship.

It was my only move in a difficult situation. If I could be the one to tell the story, then maybe the story wouldn't be spread around and haunt me. I have never been so wrong, because, as we've already talked about . . . We. Love. Drama.

THE TURN OF A NAPKIN

And this is how the weight of what happened became too much to bear. The only medicine I could find was to show up honestly, ask for the boundary of confidentiality, and honor my need to step away from our connection at least for the time being.

Everything about me was untethered, and it forced me into the corner of truth-telling and surviving without much else to choose. I knew it would make the rounds on its own anyway and wanted control of my own destiny to have the first say. Even though this wasn't something I had done.

Although I do look back on this decision and wonder if or what I would do differently now, I don't believe regret is the path to understanding ourselves and what "should" or "should not" have happened under the circumstances that cost us our friends. Our friendship became toxic the moment I spoke a truth that she was actually aware of and not disclosing the whole time. The theme of naivety and cluelessness had found a way to follow me into my adult friendships despite my best efforts, but this time with an even greater humiliation and shame alongside the injustice that none of what was happening was my fault.

Toxic things happen around us, and so often the women get shamed for the actions of their lovers, their fathers, or their partners. Not only are women often held socially accountable for harm others have caused, they are also simultaneously guilty *and* naïve.

This is another way the trend of calling our fellow female friends *toxic* is us participating in the patriarchy's work keeping us separated from each other and scapegoating our sisters and friends benefiting the actions of people in power.

Despite the fact that I had shown up for Tracy in a moment when people in her life had really fucked up, and what was happening around me was not even close in severity and true toxicity, she not only would not honor my boundaries but turned on me by sharing the information I had asked for her to keep confidential.

The hidden life of failed relationships is often where we wither away in isolation. Instead of being able to speak about what has happened with each other, we just get a diagnosis of TMJ or an autoimmune disease in the silence. We become absorbed by the loss as a deficit permanently marking our worth, and it's like we are stuck with the shame of it forever. Have we forgotten the turn of a napkin or the warmth of an inside joke?

In telling the truth in moments like this, we begin to know each other in ways we've been terrified of all along. Sometimes that means the death of a friendship, but it doesn't have to mean it's the death of ourselves or the goodness we once shared with them. And that, my friends, is stranger than fiction: to breathe the air in the space that now exists between you and the friend you thought you once knew and swallow the dark reality of what has happened in faith that you will pass through to the other side. Because encountering toxic things is a part of being a human alive on this earth.

Nothing can change until you allow your experience to matter. And this disappointment and disappearance of what we long for and need from others starts long before we ever encounter betrayal in a friendship.

WHAT'S TOXIC ISN'T REALLY THE PROBLEM

When I was kid, I could go for an eight-hour car ride with no pit stops, and at six weeks old, I woke up with dry diapers. I learned to be a person without need by holding back the truth of my own body's basic functioning. I don't know how I lasted as long as I did, but I do know that it wasn't until I was twenty-seven years old that I could use a public bathroom without anxiety enough to let my body relax to go poop. Even if I never gained anything else from therapy and the inner work of healing, all the time and expense will have been worth just that. I cannot believe how much easier my life is now. My relationship to my basic needs has changed dramatically and it's opened up, literally, a whole new world now that I can use whatever public restroom is nearby.

The relationships we have from a young age dictate our perception of what is deemed "harmless" or inconvenient, and what merits our fear and avoidance. This is not just silly, it's treacherous that normal bodily functions and desires and needs were quarantined into a wasteland of isolation and shame. Many of us have been discarding our truth and our ability to be honest with others about it, along with our needs for years. No wonder our connections remain shallow when the very thing we ought to bring each other in our faces, presence, and words is what we're told will break, burden, and block our connection. It's this false reality where what's toxic isn't really the problem but talking about it is.

A GUT-WRENCHING PLACE TO BE

With Tracy, she had her own truth too—most of which she withheld or weaponized. As our friendship became muddied and woven with intrigue, gossip, and her sharing "prayer requests" as ways of peddling private information, the scandal surrounding me brought out the self-protective parts of insincerity in her masquerading as innocence. When that didn't work, she began to change our history, telling me (not unlike Alyssa) that friendship with me was offered really because I was so needy and she was someone who could "help." Reiterating that the things I had chosen to share with her was me being dramatic and fictionalizing because I wanted attention. She had only listened because she sensed I just needed to be listened to at that moment (and not believed). When our friendship began to end, she brought up that fact—but made sure I knew it was withheld through the years. Sometimes we don't realize how much has been toxic in the connection we thought was real until it ends. Not because we are rewriting the story but because the story we believed wasn't the same one they were telling themselves in order to get what they needed from connection with us.

It's a gut-wrenching place to be. Going back through the details of this friend breakup, even as I write them today, is torturous. The pain is not as debilitating as it used to be, but the scars are still so tender.

I could make meaning of this story or even excuse her behavior and the harm she did to me. I could do a lot of things to escape the pain.

We love to find morals, reasons, and faults until we're caught up in a web of loss and our own failings—which is just the other side of the toxic friendship coin. It soothes us to turn things into lessons or lists of what to do or not do, like a couple of ibuprofen on your period, but what you really need is to let the details bleed out of your system. When we create meaning in mess, instead of seeing it as something that is part of the chaos of being alive, all we do is hasten the fallout and bypass the story. In every detail and specificity, we leave a label and a lesson, like using the napkin to make neat little circles instead of just acknowledging what's spilled—turning away from each other in the process because we no longer know the face across from us at the table.

We decide who the other person was all along. We learn and vow to never let someone "like that" in again. Maybe there's regret, but mostly we just set our teeth and start over.

It's easier when there's a mistake and someone just admits it to take away our uncertainty in the breakup of a friendship. But the reality is, there isn't. Nothing that caused our breakup was my fault. The details of my story of being called the toxic friend was really other people making broken parts of themselves my problem. But for a long time, I was so gaslit by her and others about what happened regarding who I was that I took on the blame and shame of choices other people made that had nothing to do with me. I thought, perhaps foolishly, that my honesty and willingness to engage that possibility would mean we might make it through some toxic circumstances.

The thing I did wrong in this story was talk to her about it. And when a problem between two people gets talked about, we can no longer pretend or power-play our way out of it being there.

Healing for me has been learning that going back and reconnecting to my felt experience of what happened is something that matters, because in the moment I spent a lot of my energy empathizing, self-evaluating, and pretending I didn't have any emotional needs in order to be a good friend—a good human, really. And that clouded me from seeing so much of what I actually knew to be true, that the choices made weren't mine, but I was put in the middle as the problem. Which meant this person really was not my friend, and that as much as I wanted to create room for people to give feedback on who I was, I had allowed myself to deeply connect and trust someone who was actually using me.

I remember the look she shot me the last time I saw her. Everything was 180 degrees from when we met. It was fast, it was devastating, and it took me years to let go of the thoughts that there was something I should have done differently.

Our friendship was toxic, but not because I was, or she was, but because it takes two people willing to be honest and move through conflict together in order for anything to at least repair, or end well; meaning, end in a way where you don't question your worthiness or if you were deserving of the harm you've suffered at the hand of a friend who's betrayed you.

THE MESS OF THE MESS

This kind of a friend breakup is the mess of the mess, and we don't want to touch it. We tend to rewrite the stories of lives with those we've loved, lacing the entire narrative with poison. Because when a breakup like this happens, we cannot bear to believe that there was once joy, safety, goodness, and connection between us. This is truly what is toxic because it exiles us from these parts of ourselves that felt goodness in the friendship. When we are unable to sit honestly with both the joy and the heartache, we inhale our broken friendship histories like breathing toxic paint.

While I have learned many things, and know more now than I did then, I know being honest made me the toxic friend. I also know I have to commit to honoring the tenderness of my heart in how it found safety, play, delight, inside jokes, and reciprocity in my friendship with her. Even as she rewrote parts of our story, I have to tell the whole truth about mine with her. The funny thing is, now I look like the wildly optimistic main character willing to be alive despite her revisions that tried to kill parts of me off. Our friendship story is always stranger when we don't turn it into fiction.

The hidden life of this failed relationship is where I evolved. My honesty with her led to more risks in my life that I started to take and the wild hopes I had for us to make it through the toxicity, showed me a resilience and a bigger heart than I knew I possessed.

At first, this breakup felt like I was literally dying. I unfollowed and unfriended on social media platforms. I'd avoid playgrounds, restaurants, and the gym on certain days and times of the week. I was even terrified of any make and model of her car; forever on edge about having to see the person who betrayed me so deeply ever again.

I was forced to learn how to accept myself and get used to sobbing in public places. I lived a long time as the only witness to myself and to this story. All the confusion, rejection, chaos, and fragmentation I was forced to hold on my own, because I had no other friends to turn to. Just like the ending of that movie she loved, it felt like every bone of mine was breaking, except I failed to stop the author from writing me out of her story. As a result of this friend breakup, I eventually lost my entire community. The town was too small, everyone too connected, and even if no one else knew, I no longer felt safe in the very places I had settled in to love and build with my heart and life.

Stranger Than Fiction is the story of when the unlikely optimism of a character found the author, surprised her, and changed her story from a work of a lifetime to just something with a different ending. The ending finds the main character broken, humorous, a little exhausted, but one where hope spoke—and the author listened. Her character is still foolishly optimistic and ridiculously kind for the chapters she'd put him through. And in doing so, she resigned her work to being seen as a failure when the hidden life of her character found her.[3]

THE REAL DEAL

I wish this for our friendship stories. Where we aren't compelled by the way our friendship has ended to write off all the goodness that's happened.

I guess what I'm saying is this: there's always another side—like the author meeting their character in real life. Not just to the stories we tell each other or ourselves about our ex-friends, but another side to this idea that our friendships have to be of perfect health without toxicity in order to show up for one another and ourselves.

We all say we want the real deal, someone who can be with us in our mess. But when it shows up on our doorstep and we start telling the truth to each other about what's really breaking our hearts, instead of leaning in, we tap out. It's far easier to define our friend with a story we made up in our heads the second they drive away rather than be together in the failure.

We tell ourselves, "They must be something, anything, but with me in this, they can't possibly love me, this can't be solved, I won't be understood." And the wild goose chase begins when we can't believe the belonging and presence we profess we desire, is actually in the face of a broken friend telling us the truth of their experience with us.

I'm not saying we shouldn't have boundaries about what we share with each other; I'm not telling you that you have to answer that phone call. And I'm not talking about the "friendships" with people who need you and all you need is for them to need you. Those aren't your friends, and you already know that.

It's the moment when you can't believe your friend is standing before you in the middle of some toxic circumstances trying to hold both joy and sorrow, hope and heartbreak. You know the things they're saying and what they're sharing will change everything, and you have a choice to stay or go, but more importantly there's a choice to be honest or to make up your own version of their story. What do you see when you imagine this moment? Who is there in front of you?

For me, it's a brisk spring morning standing next to my car where I had the worst moment of my life telling the truth about something that ruined a lot more before and after this moment. It wasn't even my fault; perhaps it wasn't even hers. The breeze was cold, and the sun was just barely warm enough. She didn't have a coat, and I spoke with broken sentences, through tears, and sips for air.

The last thing I said before I drove away was, "I want you to know, you are so beautiful."

And she was, as was our friendship. To this day, so much of what we shared is what I still long for with others. Both can be true.

And both have to be in order for us to connect with one another. The good and the toxic.

We need chaos-resilient friendships that don't devolve into accusatory labels or harmful gossip when someone's life falls apart. Even if the friendship needs to end, we can still honor the person we connected with and what they are going through by investing in a private place to talk about how what was happening has impacted us. Taking responsibility to heal from past friendships looks like owning what is ours, and even if nothing was our fault, that doesn't mean the person we knew should be talked about with mutual friends around us. If we feel the need to do that, we might actually be the ones who are toxic.

The other complex thing about encountering toxicity in a friendship or in your life circumstances is that when you can't be honest with everyone involved, you are set up to be gaslit. And part of being gaslit is that what you "want" has to keep changing every time what you share or ask for is disregarded or told is "too much."

Before things got messy with Tracy, I actually asked to take a break from our friendship. She refused, along with my request to keep the details private. It took a long time to recover and know that what I wanted and had asked for was actually healthy and good.

If you've been the toxic friend, or you know you've been called one behind your back, chances are you've had to disconnect from what you desire or need as being good and worthy of being respected or reciprocated in friendships.

And if you've been the toxic friend, chances are you've been called unhealthy too.

CHAPTER SEVEN

HOW TO BE AN
UNHEALTHY FRIEND

"Generally, by the time you are Real, most of your hair has been loved

off, and your eyes drop out and you get loose in the joints and very

shabby. But these things don't matter at all, because once you are

Real you can't be ugly, except to people who don't understand."

—Margery Williams, *The Velveteen Rabbit*[1]

The Velveteen Rabbit is not the story of a boy. It is the story of an object. An object that belongs to a boy. It's handed over by a tired nanny as a substitute for a china dog that can't be found at bedtime. The rabbit is much cozier, of course, though cheap. The boy plays with the rabbit by day and the rabbit talks to the toys by night. The rabbit is envied by the other toys because he is the boy's favorite, and they all criticize him for his simple appearance and features after dark—all the toys, that is, except for the wise skin horse—the oldest toy in the nursery—who tells the rabbit the truth. Together they talk about what it means to be *real*, and the horse tells the rabbit how much it hurts to become real. As he listens, the rabbit is always a little afraid of what it means to be real though he realizes he wants it.

The boy makes the rabbit feel real, and the rabbit loves the boy and the nursery. He is happy to be there with the boy, but one day the boy gets sick, so the rabbit stays with him. But when the boy is well, the rabbit is treated as a toxic contagion having been so close to the boy through all the long nights of his fever and illness. And so the boy is given a shiny, new white stuffed rabbit in place of the old one, and the velveteen rabbit gets taken out with the trash and left to be burned.[2]

What a great children's story.

SCARLET FEVER AND WHAT'S REAL

There was a time when my couch was an ever-present haven for my friends and community. My door was left unlocked and my table filled with faces of those who needed seeing: boys and girls in a community that made them grow up too quickly, while simultaneously being treated like children when they were actually adults. These friends came to my house to sit, and talk, and eat—to snuggle up together without being chaperoned, accepted in the state of themselves, finding their ways to each other and adulthood. In exchange, I had friends who washed dishes and held my babies after dinner, laughed at my jokes and played games with us that required more than two players. This is the story of our first home, the one with the plywood ramp up to the door.

One of the people who crowded around this table was my friend Melissa. We had a relationship that developed slowly and intentionally. A take-our-time-getting-to-know-each-other kind of friendship. Week by week we had a shared date at my house to talk about work (we had similar jobs) that developed into cooking experiments (we enjoyed baking) and eventually talking about the real things in life, which led to talking about boys she liked and the trauma of growing up in a restrictive community. Then there were weddings, babies, and navigating awkward conversations about sex, postpartum, life with a newborn, and conflict at home. Our friendship was like an all-natural, from-scratch, slow-cooked meal shared with nourishing connection. It was soft and comforting like a velveteen rabbit.[3]

Then came the scarlet fever—the circumstances of shame, nuance, and gossip from the last chapter bled into this one, and soon, the ways of saying "I love you, I see you, I am here for you" silently disappeared. Except in this friendship, I had specifically chosen to share no details about what was happening in my relationship, so I couldn't understand why she was backing away. I had made the opposite choice with her than I did in my other friendship where I had shared almost everything and lost connection. I hoped the boundary of privacy about my life would preserve the connection this time. I was trying to navigate the unraveling of my life by telling the truth about my circumstances only when I felt it was deeply safe or absolutely necessary.

Unfortunately, the friend from Chapter Six told the friend from Chapter Seven all the details without my knowledge. At one point I asked directly if my circumstances had been discussed; they lied and said no. They couldn't, or wouldn't, tell the truth. I felt like I was going crazy because the only way I knew things were wrong was by listening to what wasn't said. So much of human communication is nonverbal. What's unsaid can be communicated in tone, expression, body language, even silence. So when I heard the change in her voice—the time extend between texts, the disappearance of the little things we would check up on each other for—just vanish without explanation, it felt like going insane to be told that I was the one being weird for asking questions.

I remember showing up late to an event where everyone there knew we were close, and it felt like a scandal happened when I asked where she was. Everyone looked shocked because they wondered why I hadn't heard the news that she had dropped out of the group. The community knew we were close and, therefore, knew something was up when I didn't know what was going on. It was a perfect act of passive, therefore undeniable, rejection—the kind where you don't need to say or do anything to cut someone so deep. You just let gossip and the social norms do it for you.

LIKE WATER FOR PASTA

Years ago, we started cooking together at *Julie & Julia* inspired weekly hangouts. The trick was our kids had different allergies between us. So we teamed up to try new recipes of things we couldn't buy at the store that everyone could eat. We should have documented and blogged our adventures because they really were exciting and delicious. My favorite memory is the time we got lost in conversation waiting for the coconut oil to heat for gluten-free vegan donuts. We both forgot that oil is not water and doesn't need to boil for cooking. We laughed as we choked on the smoke billowing out of the kitchen window, joking that we were prepared for a medieval siege, having let the pot sit on the stove like it was water for pasta.

She gave me the name of the best massage therapist I've ever had, and we'd talk about how massage was like a therapy session for the body. She went regularly due to chronic pain, and I went for my TMJ and exhaustion. We'd watch each other's kids for the hour of time so the expense of childcare could be spared. We spent so much time together that we knew our seasonal coffee orders and would drop them off on each other's doorsteps unexpectedly with an occasional chocolate bar or flowers. And I could not get her to leave my house without washing the dishes—a never-ending task I detested that she enjoyed. In short, I let her care for me, and she let me care for her. It was a healthy relationship with a lot of reciprocity and day-to-day connection.

Sometimes I wonder if we truly make mistakes in life or if we choose to sabotage by not leaning into friendships where we are truly loved.

Is it saving the velveteen rabbit to try to rescue it from the nursery in the first place or is it better to let it burn up in the hopes that it will become real?

THE THINGS THAT DISAPPEAR

It was as if I was the only one who caught scarlet fever in the friendship. I saw the likes disappear on Instagram, the texts to her left unread, soon labeled just *delivered*. It wasn't ghosting because there was still face-to-face interaction every now and then, so I was puzzled. I hadn't said or done anything to that point and honestly couldn't imagine what went wrong, unless something was going on behind my back.

So I did what my difficult personality eventually does, and I confronted her. At this point I'd already lost one friend, a few other connections, and my life had fallen apart, so on top of that, I was desperate too. With her denial being the only evidence of something gone wrong, it was up to me to believe her words and interpret her body language.

I felt embarrassed to be desperate, to be the one who was being lied to. I felt *clueless* once again. This person who had hung out with me suddenly wasn't hanging out with me anymore, but she hadn't said anything, and I felt myself floundering. I thought this friendship would be able to make it through what was happening in my life at the time, because it wasn't connected to my problems the way my other friend was. It never occurred to me that I could lose a friendship we had so carefully and tenderly built over the years through something that didn't even involve her.

The confrontation I made was via text (which in retrospect, is always a terrible move, but it is what it is—and like I said, I was desperate). I asked her point-blank what was going on and where we were at. I told her to "just stop lying to me."

She replied and told me our friendship was unhealthy and she was "taking a step back to heal." While finally getting a real answer felt relieving, it also meant all the suspicions and gut checks I'd been trying to put behind me were true. She said exactly what I thought she already felt; she confirmed that she actually did know what I thought she knew. I had read her right, and she was aware. Which also meant that the whole time I was trying to be compassionate by holding my perceptions in check, she chose to lie and watch me go crazy.

My present self can see the setup while my past self felt like I was all, and only, the things I've been called as a friend so far: clueless, dramatic, difficult, selfish, toxic, and now . . . unhealthy. My relationship had fallen apart, and suddenly I lost the friendships I thought I would have been able to lean on in a crisis. Also, I'd just had a baby. Needless to say, it was not my favorite moment in life. Thinking about it now, this friend breakup broke me more than anything else. Maybe it was compounded, but at the same time, this friendship was unique in that it was a slow build. We literally built trust. We didn't go all in, we didn't have this magical "aha" moment. It was just a day at a time, a week-by-week connection we shared as a calm and lovely thing, because we lived little bits of life together.

Like every loss, we can connect all the details and make it make sense, but the whole point is to stop turning friends into lessons and fueling our hypervigilance by paying attention to all the "signs" that things were "going wrong." Are they there? Yep. But so are we. Them and us, her and I, separate selves always, just no longer friends anymore.

It took me literally years to recover from this friend breakup. I grieved and let myself grieve the loss like a death. Only it wasn't a "real" death—it was a living thing. She still existed, I still existed. We crossed paths, at gatherings, we now were the friend of a friend. The place I had in her life was filled for her by someone else, and the place she had in my life was filled with darkness. I was rejected by my friends when my life was the hardest it had ever been, when all the things around me were beyond answers, and I was exposed to them in that raw emotion. I was left. I became the toxic friend. I was the unhealthy friend.

A RECIPE FOR DISASTER

Social media has come to play a large part in our nonverbal communication; it's the way we tell each other what we think about each other without having to see the impact of what we have to say. If you like all of your friend's photos all the time, you also have a way to tell them you are upset without risking the vulnerability of saying so or telling them why: you simply stop liking their photos. If you unfollow, you have a way to say things are over, without saying they are over. If you block, even more so. You have power to destabilize the other person but tell yourself you're just "setting boundaries." You can say they are making assumptions about you when they ask direct questions about your intentions, because, in a way, by being covert you aren't even ready to own what you actually feel. As Brené Brown says in her book *Dare to Lead*, "Clear is kind. Unclear is unkind."[4] Online communication in addition to in-person connection has made friendships even more public and painful during a breakup.

This was a recipe for disaster. As a perceptive friend managing a passive aggressive one, I felt something was off but just enough to where I was set up to question my judgment.

I still don't know what the alternative could have been because we don't have a language for endings, for changes, a way to believe conflict can be healthy and uncomfortable. Which is why we end up gaslighting each other until the friendship breaks apart. It takes kindness and courage to believe there's another way, to believe being real with each other is not only possible but good. We miss the sacredness of holding space for one another even in failure, disappointment, betrayal, or rage. All the things we write off in someone else (and ourselves) as unhealthy.

One of the things we feel is unhealthy is neediness. It's not my favorite feeling to be honest, even after lots of therapy. Our neediness can feel unsanitary, oozy, and exposing. Needs bring up tears for us sometimes and pity from other people. But that doesn't change the fact we all are creatures of infinite need, some that can be met and some that will never be. It's part of what it means to be human.

Our needs make us vulnerable, and control gives us a way to either hide our needs or find a way for them to be met covertly. Very few of us discover how to step into the power of living with unmet needs. Very few of us allow people to be seen and honored as they show up in their neediness. As was the case for me in this friendship.

To be needy is not the same as to demand; to need is not a problem, although relationally we treat it as such. I could have titled this chapter, "How to be a *Needy* Friend," but unhealthy feels like the same thing. Essentially, we treat someone who is having a good old-fashioned honest emotional crisis as unhealthy. When really, our idea of health is to applaud those who can effectively hide that which makes us most human. Unless you're successful, and then we allow those people to be honest—or crazy—whatever keeps the public engaged.

All this goes back to how we attached, how our needs were treated as children, like me and my fear of public restrooms and of ever needing to use them in the last chapter. If we weren't allowed to have needs, or if we had to meet the needs of adults that weren't ours to care for, these opinions of our needs and others' will continue to replay in our friendships, romantic relationships, and even work environments; until we are ready to sit with where those stories and beliefs that our neediness was not allowed came from.

A SICK MIND GAME

I felt so much shame for a long time about the loss of this friendship. It felt like my fault when I knew it wasn't. It felt like my responsibility when I actually had taken responsibility. I had set boundaries (confidentiality around my circumstances), and those were violated. I had been clear and asked for direct communication and then was lied to. I risked what I needed (privacy and communication), that request was ignored, and then I was called out for how I responded so poorly. This friend breakup was a sick mind game.

In the end it hurt so much because I loved them. The grief had to run its course, and it took its sweet time. I even felt ashamed and embarrassed for how long I grieved. It took me years of showing up, of therapy, of seclusion, before I risked finding community again. I had been touched by the scarlet fever, exiled from the nursery, and left to be burned as the result of sickness that wasn't mine.

The first time a new friend came to my house after we had moved somewhere else, they brought a pot of chili with them and refused to let me make dinner. Then, after we had all eaten, they helped me with the dishes. I was fine for the evening, but I had a panic attack after they left because I was terrified. The goodness I'd found in this friendship I'd loved and lost was a part of my life again, and it was too much to take in. It would have been easier if I hadn't loved Melissa so deeply or had written her off because of how things ended between us.

I sometimes wonder if my other friend hadn't shared details about my life behind my back, would Melissa and I still be friends? I did not feel safe to share things that, turns out, weren't safe to share with her. I cared about the friendship and had a healthy (and pretty fucking accurate) idea of what I would ask our relationship to hold. For whatever reason, she decided to ask around for information I said I didn't want to share with her.

ALL THE SECRET DETAILS

Gossip is an interesting word because most interpretations of it are sexist. We don't actually offer each other the freedom to speak clearly to one another and also to honor the space we need to process things as humans—even things about our friendships with each other. In some ways, if we want to end a connection with someone and we have access to all the secret details that will kill the relationship, it might feel easier to discard the friendship than to sit in uncertainty with our friend and what they are going through.

I have a friend now who, at the time of writing this, recently lost someone close to them. This friend called me the night their other friend (who I did not know) died. I asked if they wanted to sleep on my couch so that they wouldn't be alone that night. They said yes and came over and just cried, stayed the night, and left sometime early in the morning.

To this day, while they've mentioned their deceased friend in passing, I still don't know how they died. Am I curious, yes? Could I ask now? Absolutely. But I didn't know that night how this person died so unexpectedly and so quickly. I don't think I ever will, because the details of what happened weren't necessary in order for me to show up for my friend during a terrible moment in their life.

We don't need to know the details of what our friends are going through to be with them in the middle of it. In fact, we might discover that we'd rather not.

Which is not to say that my brain is not like anybody else's and wants to start looking for how, why, and what happened in all of it. But so often, we take that information and start making up stories faster than we already do, instead of being willing to be curious.

We love the analogy of a seed in the dark when it comes to our personal growth. What if we were to love it in our relationships? That at some point in a friendship there's a messy bit, a phase that's in the darkness. There's mud, dark, rain, cold, breaking open, and lots of unknown. What if we could let our relationships just be without having to know what's happening or making assumptions about someone because of how we perceive their emotional state? And to be fair, I didn't let Melissa keep hidden what she had found out about my life either. I exposed her in the dark of her secret she kept from me, about me.

But is it possible for us to become real together? While I know it's something we each have to do on our own, does it have to mean we lose one another in the process? Or if we do have to lose someone, can we let a friendship go without stripping someone of their dignity?

While I love the story of the velveteen rabbit, what would a rewrite look like where instead of the whole nursery being carelessly thrown out and burned, his old toys and beloved companion were released and witnessed by the boy as he let them go? Instead, the boy is just given a new rabbit to play with, and we are left to wonder if he glimpsed the old one. When the boy is outside one day, the rabbit who has become real goes to see him, and the boy looks up before his once velveteen rabbit runs off. Do we also too quickly brush away the thought that those we once loved and have lost might be more real than we ever realized they were?

What if in our friendships, instead of discarding them when one person gets sick, we were to both witness each other and acknowledge the need to let go? And in that, to honor the cost and the sacrifice and love of the other, while honoring our own love even in the midst of disagreement, painful uncertainty, or near death.

AN INVITATION TO RISK

We are conditioned to live in so much fear of ourselves. We treat tension and conflict, among women especially, as a symptom of an unhealthy problem instead of a cure. The past harm in our own stories haunts and limits the ways we allow ourselves to relate to each other. We, especially as women, have been taught that to confront or fight is an indication of failure, and that to even have a need for conflict is wrong.

Why do we still hold to the idea that there is a right way to be when life is so difficult and unpredictable to live? Although we have all this social dialogue around healing and psychology, we still hold to assumptions from our past. We don't actually see being clear as being kind.[5] We don't see someone asking for what they need as healthy and well. We don't let being a mess, like *really* being a mess, be a legitimate emotional state in anything but our inspirational social media posts. It is a nice idea that we will applaud from a distance, but we aren't actually ready for that to be real.

How to be an unhealthy friend is an invitation to risk—as you deem worth it—to believe in the space in friendship for all these things. The loss of a friend in response to us actually being honest about what we are going through in our lives of course makes us feel crazy, as it would anyone.

Sometimes we want a way to get out of it by hoping that one person being real can make up for us withholding those parts of ourselves and lives. But no one can be vulnerable on behalf of you when it comes to friendship, and risking that part of yourself will not always go well.

But you can be well. Even when they call you the unhealthy friend.

CHAPTER EIGHT

HOW TO BE AN UNSAFE FRIEND

CALVIN AND HOBBES © 1993 Watterson. Reprinted with permission
of ANDREWS MCMEEL SYNDICATION. All rights reserved.

Friendship is a relationship built on uncertainty, unlike marriage or
a DTR (define-the-relationship conversation) or some other cultur-
ally described connection like "friends with benefits." A friendship
between two people exists because it's not burdened by vows,
demands, expectations, or labels. As Hobbes says to Calvin in the
cartoon above, if you need a contract for your friendship, you don't
have one. It's what makes the connection real. Think of someone
you could invite to your home this minute without cleaning up, or
who would show up at your door with your favorite cup of coffee
even if it wasn't on their way? To whom you could say anything you
needed to about the way your day had gone, good or terrible, and

175

just be heard? Who has met you with a reflection that meets the knowing of your own heart?

Doesn't that sound wonderful? Perhaps it's too good to be true if you're willing to admit you've never really known that but are still brave enough to long for it. Or maybe you're lucky enough to have someone, possibly multiple someones, in mind who you might even text to just say "I love being your friend" before you keep reading this chapter. Of course, for those of us who've loved and lost and still find ourselves in the middle of that nowhere, these words trigger the ache of knowing what goodness feels like in friendship while living lonely. It's a tender place to be, when you can imagine, or perhaps even hope for, that kind of day in your life with the friend you long for.

But what makes a chance meeting with someone into a friendship that turns out this way? Is there a secret recipe of love, reciprocity, humor, similarities, availability, and just the right amount of difference, questions, or comfortable silence? If we had it once, and things ended, is it worth trying to write down what worked and attempt to replicate it? Does going out "to win friends and influence people" get us the same feeling we want as that elusive friendship spark? Or is finding real friendship feeling more and more illusive, like the fantasy of finding our soulmate?

These were the questions I was asking myself when I met Audrey. I knew immediately that we'd be friends when in a heated debate, she diffused and softened my passionate argument about empathy in a college math class after it was met with hostility and resistance by male students in the room. She deftly and quickly translated my words on empathy into actual empathy that they could understand. This wasn't the only thing that drew me to her. That was merely our first interaction. I kept watch from a few seats away until next class when I boldly claimed the one next to her. She was elegant. She was smart. I liked that she knew who she was in a way that I wanted to too. I didn't need something from her, I just liked her, and I met her after most of the breakups you've read about until this point, which was a big deal.

A few more weeks of class went by when she found me on Facebook and sent a message asking if we could meet up for homework. We struggled through problems at the Starbucks across from a local park. It was delightful, and I showed up as myself. It was a fragile self, recovering from a lot, but that seemed to be just fine by her.

Our kids hit it off too, and our partners. A win on all sides. And because we had found each other so unexpectedly, I affectionately called her my "unicorn friend," which she resisted at first and told me to check the term with Urban Dictionary before throwing it around. I didn't bother to look it up (having learned my lesson with the word *gullible*) and simply reminded her we were both homeschooled and such definitions were irrelevant. I felt our friendship was special, and she would have to deal with that.

It was a sigh of relief after a long time of loneliness. She watched my kids so we could get away, and I watched hers. We took them to see *The LEGO Batman Movie*, and I will forever hold the image of our little people dancing to the end credit's song "I Found You" as soon as they got back from the theater. The lyrics tell the simple story of wishing for someone to find you and be with you through difficulty even as you are healing—about taking the risk to show up and let yourself be found by the people who will love you for your true self. And that from there, anything is possible.

I remember that night, I thought: "Yeah, that about sums it up."

It was picture perfect. Our kids dancing together in my living room. My boys and her boy, my girls and her girl. It's one of those idyllic memories with a haze over the image where you can play it back in your mind like a clip from a movie.

There was no reason to be scared, as the song said, and I leaned into the joy of connection with her. It's not every day you find a friend you can do life with. Especially when you were afraid you might never find one again. It felt like being a five-year-old and being told that unicorns are actually real.

When we finally encounter the kind of friendship we've been longing for, it might seem like it would be easy, like we've finally arrived home, like we've finally discovered what it means to be *real*. However, when our history of connection is scattered with heartbreak and betrayal, this is only partly true. Many of the ways we learned to cope with loss in our stories is to equate what is safe with what is familiar. This means keeping our desires and dreams for the kind of friendship we truly want always just out in front of us. In a land of make-believe where it can be true but not touched, hoped for but not felt. We want to stay where we're in control, where we don't have to be frightened that what is good might be taken away. This is because the risk of feeling joy is amplified in friendship once we notice we're dancing in real time with someone who reflects who we are and isn't a fantasy. We don't want to be thought as foolish for loving what we've longed for and thinking we could let down our guard. If we hold back just enough to stay safe, we can enjoy the other person at a distance, keeping them at arm's length from us too. We do this by keeping our desire to ourselves; that way we aren't at risk if anything doesn't go well. We keep the experience of friendship solely on our terms, for our needs, oriented to our level of comfort, and stay protected, because when we start to truly feel connected to those we love, we are exposed.

IN THE MIDDLE OF THINGS

I loved my friend and wasn't afraid to show it, but soon the coming months brought news she wasn't ready for. Her husband worked at the same organization she did but was in search of a different job. The position she held was a place where she had a voice and agency, something her previous jobs (and prior history from a religious upbringing—similar to mine) had not afforded her. What's more, she knew she was skilled at her work and earned the position she held. She was good at her job there. But when her husband was offered his dream job elsewhere and jumped at the chance, it meant the pieces of her thoughtfully built life and position at work would have to be left behind.

During this transition, she would come over to my house, sit on my couch, processing and verbalizing the change swirling around her. Her sense of integrity and love for those closest to her, alongside her own desires were now in conflict with each other. Would leaving mean losing her growth? Would she be able to keep her voice and quickly build the same rapport in a new workplace? Would staying mean sacrificing the same thing on his end?

It's the subject for another book about how women will change the course of their lives to follow a man's dream and decide the margin of the life that's left to her is enough room to bloom within.

Regardless, I knew I wasn't there to make or influence the decision for her, I was there to hold space for all that might arise in the middle of it and for her to process. Was I devastated that my newfound dear friend would move away? Of course! Did that mean I couldn't enjoy and honor the time we still had together in the waiting? No! Nor did I need her to need me; I was just grateful to be with her in the middle of things.

Being a safe person means those around us can feel what they need to feel and it doesn't factor into our sense of worth or identity. I felt that I knew this in my bones, and it was how I wanted to show up for Audrey. Having recently moved myself, I also felt capable of holding the liminal space that now made up so much of her life.

While what Audrey was processing was somewhat different from the cross-country move we had made, and the impact on my and my partner's relationship, she knew we had been through it, so that's likely what had her driving to my house and feeling safe to open up. During my family's move away from a community that turned on us and cost both my partner and me so many friendships and other connections, we had also wrestled with what it meant to create space for both of us to grow and pursue work that felt fulfilling while sharing our lives together. It wasn't easy; we weren't sure it could even be possible, but at that moment we had reached a place together where we realized our relationship wasn't worth having unless we both accepted ourselves, owned what we wanted, and were willing to engage the tension of working that out in the details of our lives. I imagine that is what drew her to my couch. In the way I was drawn to her in that math class, we were offering each other a nurturing presence, a way to find language for things we couldn't yet access ourselves.

Audrey shared and I listened, wanting to create a safe space for her to process. I was also so desirous for her to at least name and acknowledge what she wanted to happen. Did she *want* to move? Would she rather stay? What did she need if she moved? What did she need if she stayed? I could feel the futility that all of her processing of the experience of others around her would never make up for the answers within she was trying to access.

My inquiries about what she desired and the needs she had were consistently redirected or bypassed. She wanted out of the move but couldn't bring herself to let go of the familiarity of putting her desires last, such that verbalizing them wasn't even safe enough. She wasn't the oldest in her family growing up, but her role in the family was to be the mother. She reclaimed this trauma of parentification as an adult by making it her own, such that her identity hinged on this. Anyone around her who needed care would experience her as a mother. Nurturing, present, attuned, soft, and unyieldingly brave, she was a fierce and beautiful woman. These were all things she was so proud of and much of what drew me to her. She had a sense of her identity and how the role she played in her childhood impacted the way she was meant to show up in the world.

And here she was on my couch, in need of the very care she brought others so well. So we sat, she talked, and I listened, asking her questions in the hopes of making it safe enough for her to connect with the places in her that needed to speak. When deciding what to do about her situation, she knew I wouldn't let her move very far from her own heart. So she kept coming back, sending text messages after she got home each time that she was grateful for the space to process. I felt grateful too. It is a sacred thing to be trusted enough to mother a mother.

DO YOU WANT TO TALK?

One night she showed up unexpectedly with Baileys and vanilla ice cream at my house. She was all dressed up. My partner and I were watching a show with another friend when I went to answer the door.

"Do you want to talk?" I asked.

"No," she answered.

I asked again, "Are you sure?"

And she said, "No, let's watch TV."

So we all went downstairs to finish the episode I'd been watching with my partner and a friend when she called. We passed around a giant bowl of vanilla ice cream with Frangelico and Baileys. It felt a bit like communion.

A little while later, her head found its way to a pillow on my lap. Which both startled and aroused me because I have a complicated history with touch. Touch was not a thing that was safe while growing up because it was not allowed for me with those it should have been and required of me where it should not have been. As such, the only kind memory I have of touch from my childhood was trading head scratches with my mother and even then it had to be bartered for like a commodity—the "I'll scratch your back if you scratch mine" kind of thing.

So, when Audrey put her head in my lap without explanation or asking for anything just while watching TV, she was letting me care for her by simply letting me be with her. I didn't have to use words to tell her how I felt, and neither did she. Again, like a clip from a movie that you can play back in your mind, I can still feel her skin—see my hands running through her hair, sense the calm in both of our bodies, the calm my body was bringing to her body.

I had never felt that with a friend before. I had never been asked for that by a friend before. And I didn't realize it was something I so deeply longed to give and receive until that moment.

She reached her hand to rest on my thigh, drifting off a bit. The memory of her body is real enough to startle me with its softness. As someone who learned to stay out of harm by creating intimacy through language and really good listening, this moment felt good, intoxicating, calm . . . and a little bit dangerous to feel this safe in the quiet with someone.

The next morning she texted that she couldn't stop thinking about my fingers in her hair, and I felt gripped with terror that I had gone too far, or that I'd done something wrong, quickly explaining things away in my response. Now I wish I hadn't, even though there was more about that moment to be realized. I later learned that each of us had come to the edge of ourselves and what we could acknowledge about our relationship with each other.

Less than a month later, they decided to move.

CLICHÉS AND PLATITUDES

There are a number of newly spoken phrases in this generation that I hope will very soon be cliché: "You are enough," "You're not alone," "Be present," "Just breathe," "You'll find your people," etc. Included in this genre is "We need each other," and its companion "We belong to each other." While these things aren't necessarily untrue, how much we're having to repeat them to ourselves (or repost them to social media) is like putting Band-Aids on a broken arm. It shows that we are too afraid of realizing we wouldn't need to say these things to ourselves, or each other, so often if they were true in real life. But instead of asking why we don't have these things in relationship, we keep repeating them as platitudes to one another.

We do need other people, but what are we to do when we don't have community support? It's like saying "you are enough" to someone that is overwhelmed or "you're not alone" to someone who very much is.

None of what we say about friendship matters unless we actually live it. Furthermore these platitudinal ideas simply perpetuate the ideal of the "good" friend. It keeps us invested in the myth that somewhere someone can attune to our needs without us communicating, and offer us belonging without risk. Holding to these concepts surrounding connection, instead of the friend who loves us, makes our investment in any relationship safe, because we can just defect when whoever we're with doesn't provide a satisfactory solution to what we need or desire. We can move on easily and tell ourselves it can be obtained elsewhere, when in reality we were too afraid to let what we long for become real.

The troublesome thing is that rescuing our desires from these clichés will require us to risk.

This brings us to the tension in friendship we are actually in when we find ourselves experiencing the connection we long for. We find ourselves needing and being needed, we find ourselves truly belonging, and it goes against the grain of everything we're accustomed to receiving from someone.

The beauty of this is that what is harmed in a relationship (from our past), begins to be healed in relationship (in our present).[1] But the terror of it is that as our familiar history of harm starts to surface in the safety of good connection, we can become afraid of the person in front of us. We start confusing being healed *in* a friendship with being healed *because* of it. The reason this happens is because at one point, our parents should have met our needs without us communicating and given us belonging without risk. So when we meet a bump in the road in what has otherwise been a beautiful connection, we pull away instead of leaning in. Our platitudes and friendship checklists allow us to check out, instead of seeing the new narrative we can co-create in adulthood as two dynamic, unique, healing individuals.

This is one of the ways finding the freedom to show up as the bad friend changes this platitude story. We can be with others, present to their circumstances, but the integration of our stories as friends, no matter how much reflection, mirroring, and resonance we offer each other, the matriculation of all we experience together is ultimately our own to assimilate, process, and accept. No one can do our inner work for us. Some days I wish someone else could, but they cannot. Even if your experience matters to me, it can never make up for the fact that you are not allowing it to matter to you. Even if our friend accepts who we are, it cannot make up for our lack of self-acceptance. Just like drinking iced coffee is pleasant and energizing but it still doesn't count as water.

It takes two people willing to let their experience matter, and stay in that tension, to create real connection. That's real belonging, and without it we won't actually get our needs met.

RAIN IN AUGUST AND AN AMBULANCE RIDE

Our family volunteered to help my friend's family move, but the bank messed up their escrow, pushing back the closing date to a time when we weren't available. I sent a text to Audrey a week later after some of my own family's chaos had settled down, offering to make the drive and help them unpack. She said yes, and we hopped in our car with our trailer and all the food we needed to be there through the next day. It was our mission to bring whatever we needed by way of space to sleep and meals so that we could just be helpful and not add any inconvenience to them moving into their new home.

We got there too late in the evening to start, but began in the morning, setting up the living room, hanging photos on the wall, offering the houseplants a window seat. It seemed like she was having trouble deciding on what she wanted to work on, so I suggested focusing on one room that allowed for a space to be peaceful amid the chaos of moving in. She seemed to like the idea, saying that if any new visitors came by, they would have a place to sit, and she could keep unpacking the rest of the house until they were settled. It took a couple hours and when we finished, she passed out on the couch, asking me if I could start unpacking the kids' rooms upstairs. When she woke up, we went for a coffee break and to scout out the local thrift stores for kitchen cabinet handles. We didn't find any that she wanted, and as we walked back to the car, I could sense she was disappointed—and the rain clouds didn't help. But I had found my second wind with the iced latte I'd ordered despite the cold weather and hoped that a little bit more help unpacking might cheer her up.

As we started the drive back to her new house, an ambulance passed us in traffic. It had turned into one of those awful rainy days—a permeating damp chill in August, that sort of winter weather in summer can serve to make anything unpleasant.

"Have you ever ridden in an ambulance?" she turned to me and asked.

The light was red, and I said no as the sirens faded.

"I have," she stated looking straight ahead. "I almost died."

She continued, "I basically had the equivalent of a heart attack for my digestive system—and it's usually fatal."

My body was hollow and tense as she continued on with the details of her near-death story so matter-of-factly.

"I was in high school, and I got a really bad stomach flu or food poisoning and kept throwing up without any food or liquids until I couldn't get up and my mom never checked on me."

The arrow was green, and she threw me a quick sideways glance as we turned left.

"I finally managed to crawl downstairs, passed out, and woke up in the hospital. I was there for like two weeks."

The conversation was as abrupt as it seems. My head was spinning with what to do or say next.

"Oh my gosh, Audrey. That's awful. Is this something you want to talk about? That's terrifying."

She waved her hand away and said: "It's fine, I'm over it. I just wondered if you had ever been in an ambulance."

We drove on in silence. The windshield wipers screeching, the car's engine struggled up the hill and jerked along at 10 mph below the limit. She patted it gently on the dash as if to soothe the engine on, coaxing it to hold out a little longer.

Meanwhile, I was paralyzed. In what I just learned, I realized our friendship was over and there was nothing I could do. This was as far as we could go. I considered opening the car door and jumping out, taking my chance on the highway over the inevitable aftershock of what I knew she was going to say next. This was a moment six months in the making, and I now knew exactly when I made the wrong choice to risk in my friendship with her.

Don't do it, I prayed. Say something to stop it, I told myself. But if someone already thinks something about you, isn't it already kind of true?

"It may not be my place, but . . ." Her voice broke the silence and arrested me. My heart quickened and the adrenaline stole the blood from my face as it churned in my stomach.

In this moment with Audrey—the rain falling, the ambulance passing, and the windshield wipers clunking along, I was trying desperately to figure out how I was here again, how had I put pieces together incorrectly, or not, to make a unicorn real? Did I make it all up, to make things safe—was *I* safe? It was a risk for us to allow the parts neither of us knew our hearts would stumble upon as we let ourselves be together. Even still, that night sitting with her head on my lap on my couch was a place I was willing to risk being—because I thought we were risking together. I had experienced so many things I longed for in my friendship with her. I had felt connection, safety, and goodness, and offered them in return. And just like the sirens from that ambulance faded back into the sound of pattering rain, the friendship we built, vanished.

THE STORIES WE TELL

Before I tell you what she said next, we need to understand that stories live underneath almost every private thought, or relational encounter, we have.

We tell stories to each other, all the time, but not as much as we tell stories to ourselves. When we are unaware of the stories we've lived and how we've translated them to create meaning, we use others, usually unconsciously, to supplement our projected reality.

This allows us to experience the spectrum of emotions that comprise the human experience without putting our hearts on the line. And that's dark, like a forced surrogacy where someone else must bear what you are afraid to hold in the reality of your life. (Like the dramatic friend.) The truth is, until we own our stories and experience, the details we share in friendship are going to project pleasure or pain we do not want to know in ourselves. But why?

Our first formed relationship, the maternal bond, is meant to be an experience of radical acceptance. Attachment theory is the story of the myriad ways that can go wrong. And, if we remember Alice Miller, once this opportunity runs afoul, the loss is permanent. If we do not experience unconditional love as a child from our parents, that kind of love is gone for good.[2] If you think about it, it isn't boundaried or appropriate for us as adults to love each other unconditionally. It's just that we were all supposed to be loved in that way in order to love ourselves well and be self-possessed in connection with each other for the remainder of our lives. Unfortunately most of us were not, so we keep looking for others to give us the love we were supposed to have as children.

This means that for those of us without a secure attachment, the love we were made to know from infancy as a human being is gone. And no relationship afterward, no matter how fulfilling, can make up for that loss, which is heartbreaking. This is one thing to know, one thing to grieve, and another entirely to learn to live well with this permanent loss. But as long as we fail to engage the permanent lack of our parents' unconditional love, we will distract ourselves from the real connection that's in front of us, still searching for a mother's face.

As I've said earlier, what was broken in a relationship can only be healed in a relationship. I hold this truth in hope, for the most part because people with more education and the research to back it up tell me so, and because I've come to know some life-changing healing from the smallest moments through connection with others in myself. But as I mentioned before in regard to platitudes, I do not believe we can open to healing within a relationship we have structured to fill the void of unconditional love or acceptance within us. Our friends can never do for us what our mothers did not, or would not, do.

Which brings us to what Audrey said next.

THE RISK OF BELIEVING WE ARE LOVED

"It may not be my place, but . . . you ignore your children," she said.

There it was. The drop. The exact words I knew were coming, yet still completely did not expect from someone I had chosen to trust. Again. I had chosen to trust someone again, and I was betrayed.

I rode the rest of the drive in silence knowing there was no use in holding back the tears that began to flow. From the joy I felt earlier in the day, I was now as out of place from myself as the bitterly cold rain in August.

Unicorns and those who believe in them aren't considered normal. But if you were to happen upon one, would you pretend it wasn't there just to be safe? Would you be afraid of the mystery, the unexpected, the uncertainty of seeing something from your imagination before you?

When we are sitting in the brutal aftermath of a friend break-up, we try to ease the pain by answering the most human questions, but also the ones that are the most irrelevant. It gives us some relief to think through how to avoid this in friendships in the future, to chart out how it happened, what went down, where things went wrong, what we did wrong, or what they did wrong.

Essentially, once we can figure out who's to blame, we can either punish ourselves or hate someone else, adding the latest heartbreak to our history of harm and remembering why we vowed to never let anyone close ever again.

We do this to avoid the one thing we're afraid to ask ourselves about, which is our desire and how we let it be seen, how we let ourselves come alive.

A polyglot who was a regular at a coffee shop I once worked at told me that in France, when you order, the waiter doesn't say, "What can I get you?" or "Can I take your order?" They say, "Dé-sirez-vous un café?" (though I've since been told this is quite formal). But the first word is what struck me—calling forth desire, want. Almost asking, What do you desire? What do you want?

Desire is not safe, ever. It's an untamed and unconscious part of us that if you're not paying attention, you spend a great deal of your life in reckless service to. Some people try to get what they desire in ways that harm, and others in ways unaware that they're doing harm. Still, very few others can hold and move toward their desires in ways that heal. But desire that's safe is desire unrealized, stagnated, given a place to die, to suffocate, to atrophy, and here's that cliché, to be told "you're enough" or "you're not too much." Yet in our lives with lovers, we are always on the hunt to rekindle a flame, we want expansion, we want more, to keep an air of curiosity about us and the other. Desire is the place in us, and another, where we meet the unknown without fully knowing. We sense what's unseen, hear what's unsaid, and feel what's unfelt. It's this wild part of us that is not safe, but that does not mean our desire is not good.[3]

Most of us keep our relationships confined to what's predictable, only pretending we want more while making sure that any idea of what might be possible, if we truly showed up for connection, stays out of reach. We like what is "wild," something unknown and new as a concept, something for people to write about but not for us to actually risk. So when we sit down and let down our guard for something like the hands of a friend to touch our hair, the permission given to fulfill the longings of lost places in ourselves, to calm and arouse, to be safe and unsafe, the ache of what we do not have and how we wish to belong is awakened.

Most of us haven't even named what it is we actually long for in friendship, and we keep rewatching the same Disney movie for a predictable ending instead of taking the risk to discover a new story together.

But let's return to one of those irrelevant but pain-relieving questions, where we ask what happened and return to the car in the rain and the answer to why Audrey and I broke up. How I knew before I knew what she would say about my parenting and how that meant our friendship was over . . . when she told me her story of riding in an ambulance.

IN THE ARMS OF A UNICORN

When I watched her kids for the weekend, we took them to see *The LEGO Batman Movie* and had a dance party when we got home. All was well. When she watched mine, my youngest who was just over a year old, caught a stomach bug and barfed her way through all the available clothes I had packed. At the time, my partner and I were skiing in the mountains and hours away out of cell range, so we didn't see the call come through until about 4 p.m., after the worst of it had passed.

I was so discouraged, yet desperate for a break from four kids, disappointed the universe couldn't give a moment's peace—so it seemed. When I got the message, I was at the top of a ski lift, and called back immediately, ready to race down the mountain even though it would take until about midnight because of traffic to get there.

But she did something surprising.

She told me to stay.

She told me everything was fine and that my little girl was fine.

And I was so torn. Did she mean it? I sat there on a bench in the snow holding the phone with my freezing hand not knowing what to do. I had to choose to believe her, or not to believe her. But here in front of me was the kind of friendship I wanted to offer (and had offered in different contexts to others) being offered to me.

I chose to believe her, and I moved past my unbelief to risk receiving the care. Care that she was already offering my daughter, who wasn't throwing up anymore and "happy as could be in the arms of a unicorn"—which were the *exact* words she used. She called herself a unicorn and told me my kids were going to be just fine.

So is this love? Is this real? Can I rest in this way in this friendship?
I wondered. It felt tender and real, but also unsafe because it was
so unfamiliar. I took a deep breath and asked her "Are you sure?"
one last time.

My old story would have been to rush back, panicking all
the way and apologizing profusely when I arrived. Instead, I took
a deep breath and gave myself permission to let myself be loved. In
the kind of way I knew I loved. I accepted my need for the time
she'd given. I allowed it to be met. It was fragile and beautiful. And
perhaps foolish, which I now felt, in the car in August that final day.

IF YOU MOTHER A MOTHER

With all the details present, I can imagine how it might look. To
this day it's hard to not chastise myself for believing Audrey, to
not tell myself that I am not only a clueless friend but also a bad
mother. But I couldn't see the setup in those circumstances. I didn't
know until that moment in the car that her mother had basically
left her to die from a stomach flu. The déjà vu of her watching my
kids is obvious, but something no one could have predicted, something I never could have intuited. Maybe now I wouldn't have
made those choices, but that abandons the me who did. A me who
was an overwhelmed mother with no community support, letting
herself catch a break on the top of a mountain because a friend was
offering her the care she needed. It was a risk and I took it.

When we are accepted like that, the hidden and indeed core desires show through the veneer we wear everyday just to be safe. Out
of this offering of care, our friendship continued to strengthen into
the summer where she showed up to sit on my couch—or so I felt.

I let myself show up with more acceptance too, offering my ears, my hands, and my heart, in response to her talking things through, her head in my lap, and her need to be seen. Our friendship felt real and good. That is, until an ambulance passed us in traffic.

I suppose too much of a good thing can make one nauseous, like a kid eating candy. And I suppose if you mother a mother who's never been mothered, if you begin to be with them where they've been afraid to be with themselves, you become unsafe. When what you're offering someone is something they've never received, connection becomes more of a risk because it starts to open the floodgates of hope. When she told me the story of how her mother abandoned her, I knew I couldn't possibly hold it all; I never pretended I could. I knew when she told me I ignored my children, what she meant was that I ignored her, and I can now trace back the very subtle cues and requests I'd misread, or just missed. She later sent me an email saying as much and accusing me of more harm, acting as if I did not exist within basic things like boundaries of time and my own limitations. She showed her fury with me for every moment when I was genuinely unavailable as though I had been an asshole who had taken advantage of her without giving anything in return.

I began to realize I'd been assigned the role of her mother when I thought my role was friend. In showing up well, I had awakened a hunger for healing in deep places of harm for her that she wasn't ready to name, so she blamed me instead. Claiming further that in receiving and letting me care for her, she said I'd put her in a position of sharing things she hadn't actually wanted to share. She eviscerated my character and everything good I felt we had experienced throughout almost two years of friendship in a single email. It was as if all those afternoons she spent on my couch never even existed.

Acceptance is actually the worst that way. When we've learned to live so long without it, the heart goes into arrest, and an ambulance siren of accusation might be our only lifeline to escape what feels like an attack. When we were children without unconditional love, as adults, both the love and the loving are unsafe.

While the aftermath of this friend breakup found me with a little more experience this time, and I won't deny, when Taylor Swift's first single from her Reputation album, "Look What You Made Me Do," dropped within the next forty-eight hours, I was grateful. Audrey's words were a bomb out of nowhere, and I knew by this point that the kindest thing I could do for myself was not try to explain the deep pain away, and let myself process the rage brought on by this level of betrayal. I had to let the dust settle over a number of weeks and months before I could even begin to let go. It was unnerving to be here again, and so were the mind games that played over in my head that I was the common denominator in all these friend breakups. I was the harbinger of heartbreak, the failure, the causality, the problem. Clearly, I was misreading some big signs. I was a ruiner of friendships no matter how hard I tried. This time though, I didn't do more than attempt a phone call and one subtle hint via an Instagram post to make things right. I provoked her from hiding and ignoring my call with a line in a poem only she would understand, which prompted the email that came in response where she let me know exactly what she felt happened. She confirmed that she told me that story and said I ignored my children as a way of saying I ignored her, adding on that I only ever talked about me and didn't care that she had to move and blamed me for not fighting for her to stay.

I wrote one furious and one pacifying reply. Then I waited a few days and wrote a third and sent that as a middle-of-the-road version of the two. I was angry, and I was willing to work through this. I decided this time that if it was a friendship, my job was not to be safe. It was to be myself. I told the truth and my experience in response, at least accepting my own heart and grief because clearly no matter what I said it wouldn't translate to acceptance of hers. I let it be and reminded myself that if things were meant to be, we'd make it through. I didn't hear back.

In the silence that followed this time, I didn't allow the wound to remain open. I let it go. I responded by blocking her on social media, unfriending, and not contacting her again. I knew some demons had a fast pass to my heart from recent years, and nothing good would come of descending further into the realm of self-hatred than I'd already been by seeing her life online, or by taking on her fantasy of my failure. The trust was gone faster than it was built, as it always is. My phone didn't buzz and my couch stayed empty. It still hurt for a good long while, and I learned how to scream in my car and just how often I'd need to, to let it all out.

She knew my story, and I knew hers. I'd believed her questions when she'd ask to know things about me, and I berated myself for how I let her escape my questions when I trod too close to parts of her story she didn't—but apparently did—want to share. Knowing her was like having a limb grow back after losing one in a war, only to lose it again. I thought we'd be together, through a little more of this life, through healing, through this new season of finding ourselves and growing careers, watching our daughters and sons play on the trampoline in the sunshine, and taking the occasional summer camping trip somewhere between the ninety-minute drive and winding roads that separated us. I thought all this, I desired all this, and now I had to accept that all this was gone.

Here I was in the all-too-familiar space of uncertainty, with no friendship contract to say: Didn't you promise? Why couldn't you tell the truth? Don't you want to be loved? Did you ever love me? Were we ever friends? What was the point of this whole thing anyway?

Sometimes we go through friend breakups, and we make what goes wrong into a project. Searching for those easier answers, deciding what we learned, taking that sage old advice that "everyone is our teacher." Then the next time we brace for impact; if we start to feel a relationship go south, we tell ourselves we'll get better faster, we'll be smarter, our friendships will last longer. This is safer. This is more practical. But this will also cost us our joy. Some say that if you're in a car wreck and tense up before it happens, you'll be in worse shape than if you never saw what hit you. Sometimes I think about that and wonder if feeling joy that day in August before she struck me with cruel words let my heart eventually mend softer, because I wasn't braced for the impact of the betrayal that was coming. I wonder if knowing that could help us risk a little more easily in friendship, that the fear is what harms us and not the love.

We seem to think we'll find our way in friendship one day and never take another wrong turn after enough breakups. That connection is a guarantee if we learn from enough failure.

Spoiler alert, it's not. But if you think about it, do you really want to be someone else's lesson or make them your own? It's turning the friendship into disproved hypotheses on love and the connection into a contract.

When it comes to being the bad friend, and in this case the unsafe one, the real trouble I got into came from acceptance. Things had gone wrong enough for long enough in my life that, honestly, it was suicide or self-love. After this, I learned to talk without being afraid of talking too long. I asked questions without thinking I'd pried too much. And I loved, because I'd finally understood what it meant to love me. That I didn't need to guilt-trip myself on the side to keep some illusion or part of my friendship in check. I watched the way we both showed up and watered our connection with kindness. Genuinely, it felt different, it felt free, it felt real, and a little bit wild. And believe me, I was paying attention.

Except, again, acceptance is the worst. It doesn't function in proxy if you aren't willing to let it grow. When you tell the truth to yourself, within yourself, you stop being clueless or naïve, like Goldilocks or me at the lip sync contest. You stop asking what's too much, what's not enough, how can I be just right? You let all that go knowing you might get rejected for it. And seeing that kind of acceptance in someone else for themselves when you're still ignoring the little girl inside you who never had a face reflect the love you needed when you were young is infuriating. Things get quietly awkward when one person has to excuse their "messy" house and you don't, and you still invite them over anyway. When you believe your dreams and personal goals matter enough to shift your life as much—if not more—than your partner's does, and the person across the table from you drinking coffee is shrinking back from their desires. Suddenly your shared lives and love for each other makes for an imaginary conflict where there's only room for one story that has the amount of guilt that's just right. Acceptance is now dangerous, disinvited, and your life no longer is an open door to them but a forest they've walked too far into and they want to turn back.

When she told me why she'd ridden in the ambulance, I knew this golden thread of connection was at an end. I'd made the mistake months before by choosing to believe her when she told me my baby was just fine and I could take a breath. I chose to believe I was loved and receive that offer of love. And I was only wrong because it was an idea of love that was holding back a story and still living in between the lines of "supposed to." I knew when she said she'd thrown up that I had become her mother by not driving back to get my daughter at midnight that day, that I was the scapegoat in all the ways she needed to prove her hypothesis right. That she would be abandoned, that she couldn't trust me to check on her after she'd moved away, that our connection wasn't real, and that I was unsafe. By cutting me off, she could keep her assumptions safe. How interesting she chose to tell me this while driving so she would not have to see my face. I knew she'd say I ignored my children, because she needed to believe her words as true of "you ignored me." And they were true, they just belonged to another mother, hers. The accusation did not belong to me, but I was handed the blame anyway. In my emailed reply a few weeks later, I responded to this with the words, "I have loved as much of you as you would allow."

I've learned to continue on since then, with the forced amputation, and without any resolution. Having spent a lot of time looking for closure in past friend breakups I've come to realize that's not really what's needed, nor is it possible. The uncertainty that follows a friend breakup becomes part of our lives and story. I was an unsafe friend, in a reality where I didn't know my role was written for me to replay the part of someone else's trauma with just enough nuance and hidden meaning so I wouldn't know the difference and be able to show up differently.

Sometimes I wonder how often we see an ambulance when we drive. It might be once a day. Sometimes I wonder about the difference a warm summer rain makes versus a winter-like drizzle. Sometimes I wonder why my one child was the only one to get sick that week, and sometimes I wonder what if I had just driven straight home from the ski lift.

Mostly I realize that it's dangerous to believe in magical things that could be real, like unicorns.

And also, people do weird things.

Especially when they're loved.

"For love that seeks aught but the disclosure of its own mystery is not love but a net cast forth: and only the unprofitable is caught.

And let your best be for your friend.

If he must know the ebb of your tide, let him know its flood also.

For what is your friend that you should seek him with hours to kill?

Seek him always with hours to live.

For it is his to fill your need, but not your emptiness."[4]

—Kahlil Gibran

"There is no safe investment. To love at all is to be vulnerable. Love anything and your heart will certainly be wrung and possibly be broken. If you want to make sure of keeping it intact, you must give your heart to no one, not even to an animal. Wrap it carefully round with hobbies and little luxuries; avoid entanglements; lock it up safe in the casket or coffin of your selfishness. But in that casket—safe, dark, motionless, airless—it will change. It will not be broken; it will become untreatable, impenetrable, irredeemable. The alternative to tragedy, or at least to the risk of tragedy, is damnation. The only place outside Heaven where you can be perfectly safe from all the dangers and perturbations of love, is Hell."[5]

—C. S. Lewis

CHAPTER NINE

HOW TO BE A JEALOUS FRIEND

*"Our way into relationship with another is through
the avenue of voice,"*[1] page 22

". . . yet women often silence themselves in relationship."[2] page 3

—Lynn Brown and Carol Gilligan, *Meeting at the Crossroads*

I texted her about meeting up for tacos and margaritas. I knew she had no idea what was coming. I didn't know how to do what I knew I needed to do, but somehow after dinner, I finally choked out: "I'm not comfortable with your relationship with my partner."

I had waited until the very last minute when I had the check, having already insisted on paying to finally whisper these words that I could still feel I didn't have the courage to back up. It came as a shock like I knew it would. She responded in the way I knew she would: telling me that she did not intend anything, that she was devastated, asking why I hadn't said anything and how long I had felt this way.

I knew she would want details, circumstances that illuminated for her why I felt what I felt. I knew that to start giving these answers would mean I would be in a conversation I wasn't able to stay connected to myself in. I knew that now she was experiencing pain, most likely betrayal, and confusion in herself, perhaps similar to the level of what I had been feeling in silence for months.

After swearing I would never cut someone out of my life without giving them a chance, here I was, breaking up with a friend in one sentence.

LEARNING TO LEAVE OUR BODIES

When I was eleven years old, after Alyssa broke up with me via her other friend over the phone, I began to learn that leaving my body was an option that could save me from social embarrassment. The faster I could dissociate, the less pain I would feel, and life continued to afford me opportunities to practice. Eventually I became very good at being clued in to every person's experience around me but checked out from whatever was inconvenient for them about the experience I was having.

In conversations around embodiment, we can easily polarize dissociating as a lack of embodiment, rather than seeing it on a spectrum as part of having a body. Dissociating is a part of being human and is actually a valuable survival skill and resource. It gets a bad reputation because many of us with a history of trauma are stuck in it more often than we want to be. All this to say, I was still a very embodied little girl. I couldn't help it, nor did I want to. What I learned to do, however, was determine in an instant whether or not my embodied experience was something that someone wanted from me at any given point in time. The awareness of a selective worthiness about my presence became something I was very good at, because it translated into preserving connection. In fact, I didn't lose any community until I started allowing my experience to matter. From the ages of twelve to twenty-five, not a single friend broke up with me.

MELTING ICE AND MISSING KIDS

The ice had melted in my margarita to where the glass looked fuller than before. I hadn't eaten much in my anxiety, and even saying what I came there to say brought no relief to me. I didn't expect it to. I was ending a friendship I had done my very best, behind the scenes, to save. And I was aware how this final moment was as abrupt as when we met a year ago.

I had gotten a phone call from my partner telling me that our younger two kids (ages two and four) had just been returned by the police. Apparently they'd seen a bunny in the front yard and the front door was left open by my older two children (ages seven and eight at the time), so off they went on a walk together around the block in pursuit of the little creature. I had left work and was on my way to a conference several hours away to hear a favorite author speak, and even though I knew my babies were now home safe and sound, I turned straight around and went home—my body shaking and nauseous the whole way.

The conference was two days long, and the next day I had a choice to stay or go. We installed a chain lock on the front door (like the ones in hotels) that night to keep the little ones inside. I let my anxiety take a break and decided to make another attempt to attend the event.

Shortly after I arrived, I took a seat near the front when I heard a voice next to me asking, "Can I sit here?" I still have the notebook where she wrote her name and number, but as it turns out I didn't need it. It was a very niche gathering, so it made sense that we hit it off so well that we grabbed dinner together later followed by a movie. One of the things I love about our family is that we are spontaneous, and I invited my new friend over for dinner the next day. By the time I had saved her number in my phone we had already spent the three-day weekend together with plans set to meet up again soon.

From there, she kind of became part of the family. We went on hikes together, shared more meals, watched movies and shows, and had hours of fascinating conversation. It felt like having a little bit of a village. She came from a bigger family and was chill about the chaos of being around my four kids. I never doubted for a second that she showed up authentically in our friendship, and in our family. Which is what made what happened all the more devastating.

It is easy to make an enemy out of someone when the wounds are intentional.

HUMILIATION AND JEALOUSY

To be honest, the bad friend label for this chapter is one I'm still terrified of. It's scarier than being called *toxic*, because if someone calls me *jealous*, it means that I must be desperate for something I want that I'm either (a) not worthy of, or (b) unable to get, both of which are humiliating.

In fact, the friend I wrote about in the chapter on being toxic never called me that directly. Nor did she call me directly. However, after our fallout, her husband literally started calling mutual friends and told them *I* broke up with *her* because I was "jealous" my partner "had a crush on her." Neither of which were true, but like the best lies, it was sensational enough. And despite being called a lot of things, that label cut through my dissociating defenses because even though I wasn't jealous of her, I could not shake the fact that despite how I'd spoken up and shown up in that friendship, this was how someone (and now an entire network of people) viewed me. What can anyone even do to disprove that kind of thing? It's a cruel setup because the more you try to dig yourself out of appearing jealous, or saying you're not, you're seen as more desperate to get whatever it is you don't have. But staying silent doesn't dissuade people either; simply put, you're stuck with it.

That's partly the reason that my whole life I have been scared of being seen as wanting something. Because simple desires like the lip sync contest, driving the rental car, and having someone watch my kids even when they're sick turned into big problems. The freedom I attempt to reach for through my desires have all ended up costing me connection. So if someone sees through me to what I want, the chances are, at some point they will leverage that against me and the countdown on my relationships starts.

FINDING THE STORY UNDERNEATH THE WORDS

Part of my struggle in the ensuing months of this friendship was that to articulate how and why I was hurt would increase the level of awareness my friend had about my partner (a friendship that was already closer than any I'd seen my partner have, save for with me). To engage in dialogue with her about my experience and my concerns would be to bring her into a conversation I only wanted to have with my partner, and the last thing I wanted was for her to be more a part of my life, his life, or our relationship.

For a long time I could not even access language to voice my pain. I was disoriented by things she would ask for, and then receive from my partner, or by her coming over to talk emotional things out with him when I wasn't there. I was so good at hiding the reality that I was struggling, including at times with the will to live, because my soul had exited my body. Although tortured by the fact that I was doing such a good job at it, I had still convinced everyone around me I was fine. Just like I had learned to do by the time I was twelve.

At this point, you may be wondering how I got here in a friendship, or on the flip side, why this was such a big deal. For context, my partner and I grew up in purity culture, and our relationship weathered severe abuse from the community we grew up in, from the time we were sixteen until we were able to move away. One of the ways we have healed and responded to this as adults is to agree that our connection to each other is not paramount to the other's healing. If one of us needs to part ways because at some point the devastation of the sheer volume of trauma we carry (not from each other) meets a breaking point, then we will find a way to end our relationship well together. We don't need the added burden of some archaic idea of lifelong marriage stacked on top of everything else that's been placed on us. This is something really beautiful and powerful that I value deeply about our relationship. So when it just so happened that the moment my friend entered the picture at a time I felt my relationship was in a secure and connected place, I was caught off guard by how I experienced the friendship she and my partner developed.

When they hit it off, at first I was happy for him; also it was fun to have a friendship where we all connected and got along. Then it became something different where my friend, who was single and had no kids, was hanging out with my partner more than I was, having a great time. I started out by telling myself I was the problem because I had a problem with it. I kept this all inside, but I began having intrusive thoughts like, *Maybe they're his soulmate and now I'm supposed to just vanish and let them be happy together because I'm the one that's suddenly miserable and they're getting along so well.* Or, *my partner must be better off without me.* It was like someone had come in and was a better version of me than I was, and I started internalizing it as my cue to leave.

For months I continued to keep this to myself, alternating from feeling totally numb to physically nauseous nearly all the time. If I kept my mouth shut and my body checked out, I hoped I'd eventually just get over it. My inner monologue became deeply accusatory: *This is just conservative bullshit, you're being possessive, you're making this weird, you're being too critical and ruining a perfectly good friendship* and on and on until it reached the one I dreaded most: *You're just jealous and too desperate for your marriage to ever work, nobody wants to be married to you anyway, and now you know it.*

All of these accusations, of course, have origins much farther back than my relationship with my partner and obviously this friendship. Yet they still fueled the dissociation that my experience not only did not matter—but was actually *harmful* to the people I loved rather than a voice crying out from my body asking to be listened to.

This is the cost of leaving our bodies. The heartbreak, shame, and embarrassment we feel about what we want or need doesn't really disappear when we dissociate. It turns into these voices in our heads, typically directed at ourselves and sometimes others, and the longer we ignore what we're feeling, the more scathing the words tend to get.

I didn't want to be angry with my friend, I didn't want to be angry with my partner, I didn't feel anyone was doing anything wrong, but all the discomfort I felt that I couldn't figure out how to let be seen without hurting anyone else made the hopelessness inside my mind keep getting louder.

The things my partner and friend were talking about together were things I wanted to talk about. The movie they went to see together was one I wanted to go to, but we had little kids and not a lot of money, so leaving the house for time alone together was expensive. Part of how we gave each other a break was to tag team the childcare. It wasn't that we weren't giving ourselves time to connect, we were, but it's hard to feel free when you're paying $20 an hour on top of dinner trying to get a break. Especially when my inner monologue was trying to convince that I was unlovable.

This was exactly my problem, everything about where our relationship was at and the connection my friend and partner had and how that was all playing out, made sense. Mentally, I did not have an issue with any of it. My brain insisted it was me, so why couldn't my body just stop feeling the way it felt?

WAITING TO LISTEN

I could articulate so many things about what my body was begging me to say when I finally broke down. How I took on the long slow task, first with my therapist, of clearing all the urgent things away like having to tell my partner what I was feeling, or needing to figure out a boundary in this friendship, not to mention the sheer volume of guilt I'd racked up through my silence for so long. Setting aside each of the necessary questions about how I got here or what I was going to do or what problems I'd caused all became secondary to the first thing I knew I needed to attend to.

Underneath everything and waking up in my body was the desire to be seen, to no longer show up in my relationship or my friendships or my life masking what it was that I felt, where it was that I hurt, what it was that I needed, or if it was true that my experience got to matter.

Holding this desire in me was a teenage girl frozen in time at the moment where she learned to sever herself from the hope that anyone would ever come for her. A moment where she should have been able to say no and speak up, but it wasn't safe enough. A moment where she was surrounded by people who actually did mean her harm, didn't care, and did nothing to stop it.

And suddenly it made sense to me why I couldn't express to anyone how I felt about what I was experiencing in this friendship, because the way this girl inside me held on to her body meant giving up her voice.

While she was ready for me to see her, and I was ready to jump to her rescue, what surprised me was that she wasn't desperate. She was just there, waiting for me to listen.

A PLACE MUCH DEEPER WITHIN

If we look at our friendship stories as disconnected from the rest of our lives, it's like severing our voice from our body. At some point down the line, we had to compartmentalize the people we were connected to in order to keep ourselves safe.

There's no shame in that, although you likely have some; we do what we need to do to survive. This looks like allowing ourselves to think we had a parent who loved us because on some days they were nice, even though we had to manage their emotions well enough for that to ever happen. As kids we learn to tell ourselves whatever version of the story lets us stay alive.

When we start to heal and tell the truth about our stories, it is a brave thing to do. But sometimes we think the categories stay in neat little separate boxes, like past and present, mind and body, relationships and friendships. We try to keep them that way with all the labels we have for the things that don't work out. Except, as you can see here, more often than not, every experience is blended up with others from our bodies and past into the connections we have today.

The nausea I had started to feel about what was happening between my partner and my friend became a doorway to where that symptom first appeared in my story. If I had stayed with comfortable categories like "I should set better boundaries," "I should just cut her out," or the more drastic one of "I should leave my marriage," that teenage girl inside me would still be sitting there holding the key to finding my words again, probably still waiting patiently, but she had been waiting a long time. I'm sure I would have found her another way eventually, and I don't mean this to say the circumstances that led me there are canceled out as some silver lining.

What I'm trying to say is this: maybe what you're feeling toward your friend, or in your friendships, that breaks your heart, makes you want to leave, write them off, cut them out, or is so painful you don't even know how to find the words is coming from a place much deeper within yourself asking you too to listen.

The whole reason I'm laying my story out in this book is because I believe our broken friendships are holding the key not just to places we've lost in ourselves but also our way back to each other.

The wounds we carry from long ago are meant to be encountered again to be healed through connection, which will not always happen tenderly. What if instead of shutting one another out at that moment, we could find our voices to create a way whereby healing what's been broken in a friendship, parts of us that were severed long ago also get the chance to be made whole?

I know I've told story after story where this has not happened for me or those I've been friends with, but I also know I'm finally starting to own my desire for it. I believe we deeply desire friendships where failing each other does not mean we are abandoned. I deeply desire this; maybe you could even say I'm jealous. One thing I know for sure is that our world is desperate for it.

A WAY THROUGH THE SILENCE

I hated every second of the last fifteen minutes at that restaurant. Neither of us wanted to be there. I hadn't wanted to be here for months and had tried to find any other option—even leaving my marriage to escape this conversation and telling myself that it was a me problem. Some days I still wish it had been. We walked back to our cars, and parting ways crossing the street, I still remember her face, tears welling up in her eyes. We hugged, awkwardly, and she choked out, "Text me when you want to hang out," to which I nodded while knowing I never would.

I believe I will always grieve not having the words to express what I felt in the moment where our friendship was broken and the courage to risk whatever conflict might have followed. Because I think she would have stayed in it with me, and I know her friendship was worth me staying in it for her.

I wish I hadn't put her through the silence I had been made to carry my whole life.

At the same time, this is the friend to whom I am forever indebted, the choices she made with her embodied presence in my life were disruptive in such a way that unexpectedly allowed me to find my own voice.

CHAPTER TEN

HOW TO BE A BAD FRIEND

"Should auld acquaintance be forgot,
And never brought to mind?
Should auld acquaintance be forgot,
And days o' lang syne?
For auld lang syne, my dear,
For auld lang syne,
We'll take a cup o' kindness yet,
For auld lang syne."

—Robert Burns, *Auld Lang Syne*[1]

I am a one-love girl. I married my high school sweetheart and first ever boyfriend. While we jokingly (but also thoughtfully) treat anniversaries as a yearly contract renewal, he is my forever love. Just like if you grew up next door to your best friend and the two of you have been through everything and are pretty sure you'll be friends until you die, my life reads like a fairytale on the romantic side. In some ways, those are the qualifications we're told get us the "successful relationship" stamp on our identity; and no matter which way you slice it, it's still a cultural ideal. We treat people differently who have a longer stint at their previous job on their resume, who have more connections in the community, who have the most years of experience, and we ask the advice of those who have been together "the longest." It makes sense, in many categories, to hire a committed employee, to trust someone who is trusted by others, to listen to those who have studied for longer, or to ask for relationship advice from those who have "figured it out." We are finite creatures, and making the most of our time and wanting what's good to last as long as possible makes perfect sense. Or does it? Is forever really what we want, or is it leaving whole parts of us behind, unexplored, and therefore unsatisfied?

Of course, we've begun this quest when it comes to romantic love but as shown by the stories in this book, and our collective friend breakups, we haven't found the same permission in our platonic connections. What is it like to read my one-love profession above? Can you feel the comparison that creeps up around those who have "stuck it out" versus those who have cut ties and trust themselves to know when to walk away? We are pitted against each other, instead of honoring our connections as they are.

We need a world where we offer this honor to friendship, and like all those who've loved and lost, been through multiple divorces, or dated more people than they can count, we're allowed to begin, enjoy, and end with just as many humans not only as lovers but also as friends. And I'm that girl, "the friend breakup" girl. My list of messy breakups grew over the years and perhaps will continue to grow throughout the rest of my story. But what if that doesn't make me, or you, for that matter, any more of a failure or any less of a one-love person?

My friends still belong to themselves, just as much as I do, and the story of our friendships—though ended in real time—still lives on. Not because they taught me things, even though they did, and not even for the idiosyncrasies, inside jokes, or their very mannerisms woven into my expressions and voice as my own, but because of all of our failures with each other. In some sense, we are still connected to one another, because continuing to hang out in real time or being able to pat oneself on the back for showing up as the good friend does not even come close to a definition of a forever love.

Perhaps we're intrigued by longevity because it means someone endured more than what was easy, good, beautiful, or perfect. We're not really drawn to forever so much as we're all secretly wondering where failure doesn't mean something blows up in our faces or gets swept under the rug. We're all hoping there's a way for us to belong even when we fuck things up, and we actually need another person to stay through that to know it's true.

Failure is a part of becoming and being human with one another. That's not revolutionary, that's not new, we just don't ever talk about the shame that's hiding within all of us whenever it happens with those whom we share affection. We talk about the spark and the knowing and the "What? You too? I thought I was the only one."[2]

Even though we are all sick of romantic comedies that end happily ever after, we mostly have friendships that end at the first sight of an unusual conflict.

Although, as we saw, C. S. Lewis alluded that friendship is less necessary[3]; I believe that's only because we've been missing something all along that is the greatest gift we've ever been given as humans. Not just our friends, but friendship itself. Again, more than romance, it is truly the most free love in the world, because it is the only one we have that exists precisely because it is undefined. There's no contract, vows, or formality, and even in the failure, it still exists. We may say, "I have a toxic friend," but it's still a friend. That selfish friend was your friend and a bad friend is still someone who's known you in some way that others before them had not. Every friendship we have ever had is a unique encounter with another human soul and while the status of friend may begin and end, the friendship will always have a life of its own that is forever woven into your story.

This is why we must step closer to what's under the surface and hold the story of us with past friends, not in the rehashing of events or as the dehumanizing labels or "I learned my lesson" explanations. To hold the story of you and them, once together now separate, but still as friendship—failure and all. This is a holy thing. You, too, are "one love" as much as you are one lifetime. And friendships, whether they last for decades or months, have the power to offer us that love.

When we are willing to tell the truth about the friendships we've lost and our fears, or failure, or heartbreak in them, we realize that being good is not a requirement of being loved. We discover ways we are wild and dramatic, vibrantly difficult, alive in both sickness and health, safely dangerous, possessive, comforting, a bitter pill some days and sweet wine on others. We learn how to be in the welcoming arms of friendship, and in time you can welcome all of yourself even, playfully becoming not good, not bad, but simply friend, receiving and witnessing your friend as such too.

A HIDDEN MESSAGE

In the movie, *It's a Wonderful Life*,[4] there is its own hidden message about friendship. As the story goes, George Bailey, the central character, is a man with big dreams in a small town. Through a series of unfortunate circumstances, his every move to leave the town to pursue his dreams is confronted with a crisis moment where the decision always falls to him. He can choose to stay and preserve something of hope (with no guarantees) in the place he has always wanted to leave, or he can walk away and let the community fend for itself. Somehow, despite his deeply rooted and resilient pursuit of his desires, he chooses to stay every time because something has gone wrong, and although he can't fix it, he keeps showing up anyway.

The climax of the story is when someone else makes a mistake and George takes the blame for it—something that will likely send him to jail. After a lifetime of ignoring his own experience to be present for other people, he spirals and almost attempts suicide, except an angel is sent to intervene, a frail, but sweet, old man-angel named Clarence.

Clarence, knowing how George will put others before himself no matter what he has planned to do, circumvents George's suicide attempt by jumping off the bridge first, putting George in the position of being the rescuer, which actually saves his own life. As they converse after getting out of the freezing river, George casually remarks that he wishes he had never been born. Clarence, seeing the opportunity, grants this accidental wish of George's, and together they walk around the town where George has lived all his life, with no trace of him or his impact on the town or the lives of all those he knows and loves so well.

Needless to say it's a terrifying experience, to which Clarence tells him, he's been "given a great gift . . . a chance to see what the world would be like without [him]".[5]

George tries to find some place or person that's untouched by his life with the quirky angel Clarence in tow but walks through his hometown where no one knows him and everything looks different and so much has been lost, and he simply cannot understand why. Friends who were doing fine are a mess and don't recognize his face, homes that were built for hardworking people don't exist and they live in poverty instead. He has no wife or children and the beautifully restored house where he lived is still a neglected ruin. The small town of Bedford Falls doesn't even have the same name in the world where George Bailey wasn't born because he wasn't there with his small, but impactful presence showing up every day. While, during his life, he had seen no results or freedom from the burdens he had carried, in reality, his small insignificant life had amounted to more than he could ever comprehend.

It's a beautiful story that shows how the hidden life of one human holds implications, consequences, possibility, and healing that extend far beyond them.

Things eventually resolve as George runs back to the same bridge where he tried to end his life, and he says "I want to live again"[6]—not out of desperation to fix things but from seeing that the experience of his life really was beautiful even though so many things stood in the way of what he truly desired to do and become. I believe he glimpsed a life that was, until then, a failure to him, and realized he actually had far more of a story to tell. His choice to step back into his own life comes from that deep desire to live that George has always had even though he never left that "crummy little town."[7]

Clarence is gone, and the world is back to how it was where George exists. The sheriff and newspaper are waiting to arrest him at home for the money that's gone missing, until the whole town turns up at his house, pooling all their savings and spare change because they hear that, for the first time, George is in need and they want to repay him for his kindness. And the money stolen that he took the blame for is paid back and more. In the final scene, among the cash, he finds a book the angel Clarence had been carrying around on their adventure, in which is inscribed the message:[8]

> Dear George: —
> Remember <u>no</u> man
> is a failure who has
> friends.
> Thanks for the wings!
> Love
> Clarence

I grew up watching this movie every year during the holidays until my adult years, when most of these friend breakups happened, precisely because of this scene. Woven into my being, whether unconsciously or consciously, was this idea that everything else could and probably would go wrong in life, but I would always have friends. Always. And however else I, or anyone, failed, it didn't matter and you could make it through, because according to Director Frank Capra, and George Bailey's guardian angel, "no [one] is a failure who has friends."[9]

And then, as you've now read, I lost my friends. I even lost friends while writing this book. And though I do have some new and beautiful friendships now, I wonder, *Am I a failure?* I lost, what felt like to me, everything *and* the people who mattered most to me. There was nothing I could do about it. Then I moved somewhere else, and I lost all my friends again. What on earth was wrong with me?

I can't show you how to be vulnerable, or even how to be a friend so this will never happen to you (spoiler alert: no one can, and whoever preaches otherwise is marketing an ideal).[10] What I can show you is that what happens after you're vulnerable is okay. Even if that means (or meant) all your friendships have ended. And that's the only way all the stigmas, and systems, and labels, and secret agendas around friendship are gonna go away. Because it is our responsibility to show each other that being good is not a requirement for being loved, by letting ourselves off the hook first.

I believe we can change the world if we start letting that freedom become real in our friendships, to no longer demand only "good" from each other, and instead to embrace failure as part of what connects us.

It will take time and dedication for us to collectively reduce the stigmatization of conflict in friendship (especially among women). For us to recognize in our relationships with each other that real presence and investment looks like taking that kind of risk and showing up in tension for the beauty it is. For us to believe that we can have conflict and still be well, we need to commit to learning how to have conflict the same way we have committed to learning how to be vulnerable.

Instead we do all these weird things and are subliminally told to label past friends (and therefore parts of ourselves) into oblivion. We have to stop turning people into lessons. We need to recognize that belonging includes letting our past friendship stories matter, not as good or bad, but simply as ourselves, simply as friendship.

The story of *It's a Wonderful Life* isn't really about friendship, but when I finally decided to watch the film again with all my friendship failures, I was surprised to see Clarence's inscription—this time with a hidden message. A bit like the way you can reread a poem and see something new. He's underlined only two words "no" and "friends" with the message of no man being a failure. Whether it really meant something or not isn't what matters. In that moment, something clicked, and I was free to see all that had happened in my friendships, failures, and loss of them as a part of who I was and who they were, and that—that—*is friendship*.

And friendship, whatever form it takes, even with betrayal, can hold it all, beginning to end, no matter what happens. This is friendship, and within all that happens is a hidden life we may not yet see. Like George Bailey, who was given the chance to never have been born, I was given the chance to see what life was like with no friends. Where I was forced to retrace my steps in friendship and in my own heart, and see the places that were missing, that were different, that were wounded, that were a failure, that were beautiful, that were gone, that might have been, that would never be, and in so doing was startled at how my own presence and theirs told more of the story and the impact of our friendship in the absence.

And then, from this place, I learned to live again.

This time with a deep knowing of the sacredness that every lost and failed friendship, of having no friends and failing again, brought me to a place of seeing this hidden life. Where if I had just labeled them to move on . . . I would have missed it.

Since then, I've still had to break up with friends, and I've been broken up with. While that part is still painful, it also now gets to be curious and wild.

I could continue to write about the friends who have moved in and out and through my life. Holding connection in this way invites us to friendships as part of an ever-unfolding story calling us to a continued understanding of who we are and what it means to be human together. I have had totally new experiences in friendship, including being honest about how I'm really feeling, as well as engaging my own failures. It's in some ways, scarier and more difficult than what, up until now, has been familiar. I've watched my friends be clear with me, and me be clear with them. I've listened to how I've made them feel and what I've offered in return as reflection, and apology has been—dare I say it?—enough. There's been mistakes on my, and their, part, sometimes of confusion, and still it is just allowed to be what it is. They are they, I am I, and we are we. This, for me, is new friendship ground.

The more tension we risk with someone, the smaller the space needs to be for us to trust enough to lean in. Friendship holds such a space. We are built for this as a part of belonging, and when we know that it is okay if things end (or even if they do not), the other side of even the smallest conflict will be a different connection than we knew before. To step into a friendship after a time of deep loss and loneliness is to say yes to life, to say "I want to live again"[11] like George Bailey, in a new way.

Krista Tippett, in an interview with Mary Catherine Bateson discusses an observation from Mary's mother, anthropologist Margaret Mead, that "everyone has three marriages even if it's to the same person."[12] I believe with our friends, we are invited to countless iterations of a friendship as a dance of humanness with another person. That friendship is what is constant, and our friends are changing partners in that dance or actors on a stage as we each play different roles in each other's lives at different times. We may even change partners and find a new role *because* we fail them, and yet, that does not mean we are failures or inconstant if we do.

Being the bad friend means understanding that failure is a part of our need for connection, our need for each other. It's recognizing that what is unfulfilled or lacking or messed up in our friendships is just as important as what is good. This is the place where you become *real*, like the velveteen rabbit. You become someone who is settled in the present belonging. They might never even know how much you love them, but it doesn't matter, you just live it. You are the one-love friend, and so are they, even if they don't know it yet.

Being the bad friend means you have reckoned with yourself and will no longer abandon yourself, no matter what you are called. Even when you're sent that final text because you aren't behaving as they think you should because of who they have decided you are, you will be present as yourself. Even if something you're doing needs to change, being the bad friend means you hold that responsibility as yours and you're able to see yourself as just as human as the person in front of you—not better, not worse. Being the bad friend means you aren't looking to prove how much you love them, you simply show up. It's hard when they don't see the hidden life underneath, but that does not make your presence any less beautiful.

You realize it's not about being good.

What's interesting is for years we exclusively sent men into battle and forced the women to stay home. In some ways, we can see men as the ones being at war, but the reality is—and as this book shows—we have found our own ways to fight to the death in our friendships, with glances, social exclusion, passive aggressive power dynamics and sometimes words.

People-pleasing and the assignment of friendship, the making, being, having, of friends, has been our battleground. When women are at war, it has to look like cordiality. Thin smiles or tears and, my god, the awkwardness. These are all the things we are afraid of because we aren't allowed to have tension with each other unless we want to risk being excluded.

I don't often think of things I would say to my younger self, mostly because the more inner work I do, the more proud of her I feel allowed to become. She has really shown up, and it's honestly her advice I want to hear.

But something I think I would say now is how proud I am of her tears on the phone that day with Alyssa. That it was okay for eleven-year-old me to be so astonished and feel everything I felt. That I wasn't responsible for how Alyssa felt about telling her truth to me because my reaction was my truth and we brought what was real for both of us to that moment. In some ways, each chapter has been a way to tell my younger self—and I hope you hear it for yours too—that I am proud of her for showing up even as she was called every name she has been called as a friend. Because through it all, she was still a friend. And you were too.

Her cluelessness is playful, her drama is fun, her difficulty intriguing, her selfishness, integrity, her toxicity a marking of what's sacred and what does not belong to another, her unhealthiness a risk that freed her from having to be safe or good, and her jealousy a commitment to coming back to herself and her desires and her body.

I won't get a George Bailey view on what my friends' lives would have been without me. I don't think I'd want one, to be honest. I don't believe we have to suffer to become who we truly are. Suffering is where we're invited to heal and be cared for, not where we have to inspire. I do, however, believe that whatever we have been to each other in friendship never makes us any less human and that the invitation is always to see what has been brought to life in us through it, which is hidden underneath the label of failure. Knowing that to write off the beauty of one person in our past is to limit our delight in our future.

What's also just plain fun about this as we show up with our true selves, faults and all, and accept people in the same way, is that those who have wronged you cannot handle being honored. The acceptance of yourself is a prerequisite to owning your failure or asking others to do the same. To offer this to ourselves and each other is true kindness, and it is always surprising to someone when we don't respond to blame with shame—inviting them instead back into the friendship dance through engaging their stories or freely taking ownership of ours.

Women especially, for centuries, have lived generations of life-times bound to certain relationships: enslavement, servitude, marriage, cruel mothers, societal roles, inferiority, subjugation, rejection, and disqualification. They found a way, despite such roles, to usher in change and freedom for those who came after them. We stand on their shoulders and hope to follow in the courage of their footsteps.

There is another place, though, where we are bound. In finding a way forward through a world against us, we have had to rely on each other. Such support and connection is sacred, and I hope it always exists. Yet, for us to remain tied together without continuing toward freedom in ending friendship well is to hold ourselves back from further evolution, individually and collectively.

More than just the nicety of "people come into your life for a reason"—wrapping up a messy ending with a neat little bow of meaning—friendship breakups are our intuition speaking the truth of ending once again in our lives. The word *friend* holds the word "end" within itself, and it's time for us to embrace together the right to leave our friendships without the threat of shame. The same freedom that we have fought for women who leave their lovers. We are not meant to be bound to one another beyond what our hearts feel called toward.

To end and, even more so, to end well with a friend is an act of defiance that forever is not a vow we must keep to anyone or anything at the cost of ourselves. Sometimes it takes an ending with a friend we thought would be there forever to realize that the people we thought we were supposed to be there forever no longer have to be given our time, our longing, our desire, our desperation, or our life.

We find that we are free.

Though we might be labeled, marked, or cursed as we go, the words do not stick like they used to because we have done the labor of birthing ourselves through the pain of the breakup with a friend. In doing so, we become more than resilient; we are committed to the one within that we do have a lifelong relationship with.

Through all the searching for the right way to do things, or "how to be" when it comes to friendship, we miss the gift that we are giving one another back to ourselves. Every time we let go, every time we hold back or step back, we are releasing being a mother and offering the presence of a friend. We are not here to heal the childhood wounds of each other, though we will. We are not here to accept the selfhood of each other, though we do. We are not here to provide a love that lasts forever . . . and yet it shall.

It's at the end of a phone call that's gone on just a bit too long where we say, "I'm gonna let you go."

A friend breakup is a holy thing. It is the one relationship we cannot live without and yet will find more of in others and can discover again and again.

Friendship is the connection that ushers us into the liturgy of endings in what it means to be alive, to be human, freeing us from the impossible demand of being good.

The end

ACKNOWLEDGMENTS

Before I knew I wanted to write a book on friend breakups but after I had lost all these friendships, I would pour over the names in the Acknowledgments of every book I read, often holding my breath, sometimes with tears. I would see the names of people I did not know and the words that accompanied them and wonder how it was that someone could be so loved. The second thought to occur to me after the idea for this book and its title was the lack of friends I had and the fact that I would need friends in order to write this book. What a conundrum.

Now, here I am, five years from that moment. As I write this, there are six unopened text messages on my phone, two from friends, one from family—all answering or asking or offering something that will help put the finishing touches on this book. I had dinner with someone last week who has patiently known me through this entire process, and this entire project would not exist were it not for a friend I have not seen in far too long. This book wrote me out of loneliness and into more of an understanding of love than I knew was possible. I wondered if it would, and as I sit here typing, I am filled with wonder that it has, and I'm wondering as I hand it off to you—my dear readers—how it will, now, for you. After enduring all the heartache of the names we have been called as friends, I hope you too will remember to write down the names of those who've loved you through more than what was easy and good. Here is my sure-to-be-incomplete but beautiful list of the humans who helped me write this book.

First, my friends. Shel, thank you for telling me I had an outline when I didn't know it and for always reminding me I have everything I need—especially when I doubted myself or was asking for help when I ought to look inward. Thank you for your encouragement and urging of me to do the work. Amy, thank you for being the friend who I can trust to pick up the phone or not, for knowing me through every single story in this book and loving me all the same. You're the closest thing I have in this world to a sister. Thank you for teaching me how to cook eggplant and sing my heart out, and reminding me I'm worthy of belonging no matter how broken I feel. Lauren, thank you for every homecooked meal and invitation to your house. The joy of living near you, our walks around the pond, along with your ever-kind and curious questions throughout this project have been a place where I could catch my breath, embrace the present moment, and return to whatever it was I needed to do next with a renewed heart. Your presence is a gift to this world. Thank you for simply *being* with me. Gina, many of these words were written sitting across from you at a handful of coffee shops. Thank you for your wisdom as the writer who is further down the road than I and for generously answering all my questions and curiosities. For the hours we spend talking before writing, I find that time itself expands in how the words flow out of me after connecting with you. I'm honored to know you, ever grateful our paths crossed, and can't wait for the world to read more of your words. To my beloved friends and beta readers Ellie, Erin, Tess, thank you all for taking on the monumental task of reading this book in its messiest form. Your feedback offered me the eyes, input, and extra pep in my step needed to finish this process. Ellie, thank you for listening to me in some of my most raw moments, and for the treasure of every Tuesday morning conversation with you. You've changed the way I see the world and widened my heart through your brilliance and friendship. Erin, thank you for reminding me not to "hedge" myself off from help, and for the transformative encounter of your friendship. I look forward to the years of reading your poetry and hearing you read it. You remind me to play and speak my mind. Tess, you know me at a depth more than most. Thank you for being a witness to me in the darkness, for calling me out when I need it, staying in tension, and lingering in beauty with me. You bring life to every room and relationship you are in, and I am so glad we randomly ended up as roommates in Seattle. We had no idea what we were getting into, and I wouldn't change a thing. I love you. Jessica, thank you for delighting in my excitement when I first had the idea for this book. You told me everything I didn't know I needed to know about self-publishing, and I've leaned on your wisdom as well as confidence in who I am more than you know. I miss you and hope to see you in real life again soon. Lorri, you too have known me since the beginnings of this project. Thank you for asking me the right questions and listening and believing in me. You will always be my Spark Mom, and here's to many more years at the Inn together. Drinks on me. Maggie, thank you for listening to me cry about this book and for your words to me that helped me make it to the finish line. Our FaceTime chats are my favorite, and I am so glad I stole your seat at the community dinner where we met and became friends.

You're stuck with me for good despite what this book says. Page, thank you for making me a better writer and for giving me solid feedback on other projects even though I get mad and for still being my friend. I look forward to our future careers and connection with each other. You bring people back to themselves, it's like magic. Abby, I don't know another way to say it, but sitting with you, my soul feels at home. Thank you for holding space for my insecurity and helping me find my voice. You are a wise and powerful woman, and I am grateful to know you. Danielle, thank you for your persistent urging of me toward school and asking me how I am and where I am on what I have said I would do. Your voice and presence have changed my life as I know they have many others. Thank you also for looking over certain sections of this book for me to make sure what is written is said well. Chris, thank you for listening to me read and reread some paragraphs until the phrasing was just right. And for reminding me that I need Christmas. Truly in awe of you and so grateful for our friendship. Dillon, thank you for being my friend and helping me see how I impact the people I care about—for good and for ill. Your kindness and acceptance of me, and my whole family, has changed me.

Second, my teachers. Amy Day, and friends, who created the space that was Haven Yoga; your work and guidance and welcome let me come back home to my body and soul. Whenever I wonder, *How is healing possible?* I'm brought back to the memories of being on the mat in that upper room. Sarajane Case, you ask the right questions at exactly the right time. Your work continues to inspire me, and I'm ever grateful you asked me: "Why aren't you doing that?" so that I could give myself permission to start the work that eventually led me here. Peter Rollins, thank you for creating space for people like me to connect with others who can help them do what they want to do, and for the generosity of your questions, critique, and encouragement along the way. To all my facilitators, group members, and the teaching staff at The Allender Center, thank you for showing me how to read story—first and foremost, my own, and for allowing me to know yours. I am forever changed because of you. Cathy Loerzel, thank you for who you are and for the transformative gift it has been to sit under your teaching, and thank you for seeing me in both my brokenness and goodness. I am who I am today because of you, and I know I'm one of a multitude who say the same. And finally my therapist, thank you for the long years of faithful presence you have and continue to offer me and for holding my stories of shame, heartache, desperation, and desire with honor, honesty, and hope. And for making room for all of my parts to be known by my self.

Third, my editors. Megan Febuary, you have an ability to see the beauty and call it forth in the midst of a lot of chaos. Thank you for being a safe place for my *sacred* (as you say—not *shitty*) first draft to be seen, for asking me to dig deeper when I didn't think I could, for giving your honest opinion, and leaving room for me to find my way. Thank you too, for a beautiful cover. This book would not be here were it not for your guidance, care, and edits. Gina DeMillo Wagner, thank you again—here for your feedback on chapters, I continue to learn so much from you. Thank you too, to my trilingual cousin for helping me with the translation of French. Carly Catt, Susi Clark, and Ellen Polk, thank you for taking on the final tasks of copy editing, layout, and proofreading this book. I am also truly grateful to every person who helped me obtain permissions for the quotes and sources used in this book.

Four, my helpers. To my nanny, thank you for all the care tasks you do and for loving on my kids and making sure they have what they need and get to play. Finishing this book has been far more relaxing thanks to your care of my family. Thank you also to whoever makes the frozen tikka masala for Trader Joe's, every DoorDash driver who has delivered dinner in the last five years and the people who made the food, the professionals who have cleaned my house, the baristas at Sweet Bloom where I wrote most of this book, and the bartenders at Arvada Tavern where from the early days of this book's ideation I would meet with other creatives in the back room.

Last, and best, my forever loves. To my children: In many ways you did not choose to have a mom who wrote a book. All the hours I have been gone and weekends I've been unavailable and pancakes we haven't made and snuggles we haven't had and moments where you needed me and I wasn't there is just some of the cost you've paid for this work to exist. Rather than a thank-you, I know some repair is in order and ongoing, and I want you to know I see what you've lost and suffered without a choice on my behalf. You too have been some of the closest witnesses to the daily grief of having a mom who lost friends and having your own grief at how that meant you lost friends too. I am more heartbroken at this loss for you and failure on my part than anything else. And thank you for your persistent desire, requests, and demands that we spend time together. You bring me back from distraction, and I'm really always in awe at the power of your acceptance of my presence as who I am as enough. Sitting with you on the couch, going for a walk or on an adventure is truly my favorite. Someday if you read this book, I hope the nurturing you need is something you look back on as having received and for where it is lacking that I may have the honor of acknowledging that so you do not have to hold it alone. I delight in the friendships I see you developing and am so proud of (and inspired by) the ways you are already working through conflict, saying no when you need to, and saying hello to everyone as we walk you to school. You are the coolest kids I know, and I hope I grow up to be a cool enough mom so we get to be friends.

Nathan, I think I finally get it when people say, "There are not enough words to express my gratitude," because it's true—there aren't. You have made space for me, you have listened to me, you have valued my voice, challenged it, stayed in conflict with me, delighted in me, believed in me, and loved me. In all the long years of not only writing this book, you have been the arms that have held me as I've wept my way through every friendship heartbreak and more. All the time and money it has cost for this to happen, you have gladly made room for—even when I was scared to accept it. You have taken on all my care tasks, mental load included, and let me say no to any of your requests for help as much as I needed to in order to finish this work. The promise I have kept to myself in writing this is encompassed by the love you have shown me through, around, before, and beyond it. Thank you for reading my beta draft and wrestling with me in the edits; for telling me when my sentences don't make sense and then waiting patiently through the madness until I found the right words. I can't afford to quote Taylor Swift here, but you know that from the moment I saw you I knew we would end up together and that my pain, my joy, my delight, dreams, and "very"-ness could all belong with you. Building a life with you, healing alongside you, creating in our own ways separately—together—for all the years we've had and are ahead is "the best day that I have." You are my forever love, my dearest friend, the Sam to my Frodo, and Kevin to my Nora. I'm yours. For reals. For always.

ENDNOTES

EPIGRAPH

1. Mary Oliver, "Wild Geese," In *Devotions: The Selected Poems of Mary Oliver* (New York, NY: Penguin Press, 2017), 347.

CHAPTER ONE

1. *The Breakfast Club*, directed by John Hughes (Universal Pictures, A&M Films, and Channel Productions, 1985), 1:22:48.
2. Brené Brown, "People Are Hard to Hate Close Up. Move In," *Braving the Wilderness: The Quest for True Belonging and the Courage to Stand Alone* (New York, NY: Random House, 2017), 86–87.
3. Brown, *Braving the Wilderness*, 86–87.
4. This concept and phenomenon has been studied and articulated in many ways by psychologists, therapists, philosophers, and others. Shame quickly becomes a collective experience that we all want to get out of; or in humiliation: the shame felt by one person is on display for all. In either case, shame never just arrives from a single moment but rather includes our whole history with it.
5. Sometimes the necklace splits the words "Best Friend" equally, in which case the receiver gets the one with the letters "st" above "end." Either way it spells out something of a role, and perhaps a prophecy, for the fri"end"ship.
6. C. S. Lewis, *The Four Loves* (1960; reis., New York, NY: HarperOne, 2017), 114.
7. C. S. Lewis, 74.
8. John O'Donohue, "Prologue," In *Anam Cara: A Book of Celtic Wisdom* (New York, NY: Harper Perennial, 1997), xvii.
9. C. S. Lewis, 74.
10. Both the work of Dr. Dan Allender and Brené Brown, in her TedTalk on shame, explore this in depth and have influenced my understanding of this concept.
11. Brown, 86–87.

CHAPTER TWO

1. Leo Tolstoy, "Leo Tolstoy > Quotes," Goodreads, accessed March 23, 2023, https://tinyurl.com/4hp3xcst

2. Clarissa Pinkola Estés, *Women Who Run With the Wolves* (New York, NY: Ballantine Books, 1992), 16.

3. This is a philosophical concept from the work of Peter Rollins and Jacques Lacan.

4. Bessel Van Der Kolk, *The Body Keeps the Score: Brain, Mind, and Body in the Healing of Trauma* (New York, NY: Penguin Books, 2014), 43–44.

5. This concept is from the work of Dr. Dan Allender and The Allender Center.

6. Indigenous people and other collectivist cultures have very different structures around conflict as well as ways to restore connection when relationships have been disrupted. Colonization seeks to strategically eliminate any way of life where people are free to be together and become who they are in community. These concepts have been extensively written about in many ways (either generally, or specifically relating to friendship) by authors such as Paulo Friere, Ada Maria Isasi-Díaz, Mary Kawena Pukui, and Joy Harjo. Patriarchy also seeks to prevent women from being able to have conflict or access to their own voice, which impacts community formation as well. This concept is powerfully written about in the book *Meeting at the Crossroads: Women's Psychology and Girls' Development* by Lynn Mikel Brown and Carol Gilligan.

7. This is a concept from the work of Dan Siegel who talks about the impact of the narratives we generate about ourselves on a neurobiological level in his book *The Developing Mind: How Relationships and the Brain Interact to Shape Who We Are.* Brené Brown also uses this language when talking about the impact of shame and blame on relationships.

8. J. R. R. Tolkien, *The Lord of the Rings: The Fellowship of the Ring* (1954; reis., Boston, MA: Houghton Mifflin, 1982), 10–423.

CHAPTER THREE

1. Isabelle Tinati, (@isabelletinati), "No detail is too small tell me literally everything idc #tea #fyp #drama #MakeItMagical #Artmas" (TikTok, December 18, 2020).

2. Frederick Buechner, *Wishful Thinking: A Seeker's ABC* (New York, NY: HarperCollins, 1993), 39.

3. Brown, *Braving the Wilderness,* 86–87.

4. Buechner, *Wishful Thinking,* 39.

5. I wish to recognize Brené Brown uses the metaphor of a critic in her original TedTalk. My analogy, however, is about the function of criticism in friendships through the roles we cast each other in and how we use those positions to hide from something that reveals truth to us about ourselves. We either witness and remain present, or we watch and judge.

6. This concept is from Cathy Loerzel, MA, and Dr. Dan Allender's work through The Allender Center.

7. Esther Perel, "The Secret to Desire in a Long-Term Relationship," filmed 2013, in New York. TED video, 3:09–3:45, https://www.ted.com/talks/esther_perel_the_secret_to_desire_in_a_long_term_relationship/transcript?language=en.

8. Buechner, 39.

CHAPTER FOUR

1. Esther Perel, "Famed Relationship Therapist Esther Perel Gives Advice on Intimacy, Careers, and Self-Improvement," YouTube, uploaded by Summit, February 13, 2019, 1:54, https://www.youtube.com/watch?v=QFwWvr1YUjA

2. Dan Allender, "The Marriage Conference," (teaching session, Highlands Ranch, CO, March 4–5, 2016).

3. This is a pre-pandemic rate from five-plus years ago.

4. Perel, 1:54.

5. C. S. Lewis, *The Four Loves* (1960; reis., New York, NY: HarperOne, 2017), 100.

6. Ana Maria Spagna, *Uplake: Restless Essays of Coming and Going* (Seattle, WA: University of Washington Press, 2018), 127–128.

7. Spagna, 128.

8. Laurence Gonzales, *Deep Survival: Who Lives, Who Dies, and Why* (2004; reis., New York, NY: Norton, 2017), 127.

9. Gonzales, 127.

10. I was introduced to, and learned, this concept through the work of Cathy Loerzel, MA at The Allender Center. The original source is from psychoanalyst

Karen Maroda's work. You can read more about this concept as it is applied in psychoanalytic theory in her latest book, *The Analyst's Vulnerability: Impact on Theory and Practice*, in the chapter "Deconstructing Enactment."

11. The name for this in psychoanalytic terminology is *projective identification*.

12. Emily Dickinson, "*I dwell in Possibility–*" public domain.

13. Spagna, 128.

CHAPTER FIVE

1. P.D. Eastman, *Are you my mother?* (1960; reis., New York, NY: Random House, 1988).

2. Yung Pueblo, *Clarity & Connection* (Kansas City, MO: Andrews McMeel, 2021), 102.

3. C. S. Lewis, *The Lion, the Witch, and the Wardrobe* (New York, NY: Macmillan Publishing, 1970), 16.

4. David Schnarch, *Brain Talk: How Mind Mapping Brain Science Can Change Your Life & Everyone In It* (Evergreen, CO: Sterling Publishers, 2018), 204–214.

5. Richard C. Schwartz, *No Bad Parts: Healing Trauma and Restoring Wholeness with The Internal Family Systems Model* (Boulder, CO: Sounds True, 2021), 14–17; Walt Whitman, "Songs of Myself, 51," public domain.

6. This is not to say that giving is not also deeply vulnerable; however, in Western culture (an individualist and capitalist society), giving is often used as a power dynamic.

7. Attachment Theory was developed by John Bowlby and Mary Ainsworth. My understanding of this theory continues to grow, and this overview is from many years of psychoeducation from my own personal therapy, teaching from Abby Wong-Heffter, LMHC, The Allender Center, a variety of books, namely *Becoming Attached: First Relationships and How They Shape Our Capacity to Love* by Robert Karen, and other research articles. This overview is written as a summary of my learnings from a multiplicity of resources through the years.

8. Dan Siegel, *The Developing Mind: How Relationships and the Brain Interact to Shape Who We Are* (New York, NY: The Guilford Press, 2020), 190–191.

9. This is from Donald Winnicott's concept of the "good-enough mother," and the percentage is from his research on what children needed to securely attach. His book *Playing and Reality* explores this in depth.

10. Abby Wong-Heffter, LMHC. For more information on her and her work, visit https://www.yellowchairconversations.com.

11. It is important to note that disorganized attachment does not immediately mean there is childhood trauma, even if it is more likely, Siegel, 218.

12. Alice Miller, *The Drama of the Gifted Child: The Search for the True Self* (1981; reis., New York, NY: Basic Books, 2007), 44–45.

13. Miller, 51.

14. Peter Rollins, "A Guide To Making Love | The Commentary," YouTube, March 15, 2019, 8:58 to 10:12; 13:15 to 13:26, https://www.youtube.com/watch?v=bUoACXWexZQ.

15. Here and in the rest of the book I will use the word *mother*, not as a gendered term, but to illustrate the role in development that nurturing plays in our lives. This can be fulfilled by anyone of any gender identity. In terminology it is care we have historically identified archetypally as feminine or maternal, whomever it is from.

16. Peter Rollins, *The Fidelity of Betrayal: Towards a Church Beyond Belief* (Brewster, MA: Paraclete Press, 2008), 13–25, 181–184.

17. Clarissa Pinkola Estés, *Women Who Run With the Wolves* (New York, NY: Ballantine Books, 1992), 303–304.

18. Pinkola Estés, 244.

CHAPTER SIX

1. Fred Rogers, "Fred Rogers > Quotes," Goodreads, accessed February 27, 2023, https://tinyurl.com/mr2h43ps

2. *Stranger Than Fiction*, directed by Marc Forster (Columbia Pictures and Mandate Pictures, 2006).

3. Forster, 2006.

CHAPTER SEVEN

1. Margery Willams, *The Velveteen Rabbit* (New York, NY: Doubleday, 1922) 5, 8.

2. Williams, *The Velveteen Rabbit.*

3. Williams, *The Velveteen Rabbit.*

4. Brené Brown, *Dare to Lead: Brave Work. Tough Conversations. Whole Hearts.* (New York, NY: Random House, 2018), 48.

5. Brown, 48.

CHAPTER EIGHT

1. This concept is not original to me and is stated by many therapists, authors, and creators as a general premise of healing. We heal in connection to one another. However, the application and articulation of this idea as related to friendship is my own.
2. Alice Miller, *The Drama of the Gifted Child: The Search for the True Self* (1981; reis., New York, NY: Basic Books, 2007), 44–45.
3. C. S. Lewis, *The Lion, the Witch, and the Wardrobe.* (New York, NY: Macmillan Publishing, 1970), 75–76.
4. Kahlil Gibran, *The Prophet* (Urbana, IL: Project Gutenberg, 2021), https://tinyurl.com/yc2rcmxu
5. C.S. Lewis, *The Four Loves* (1960; reis., New York, NY: HarperOne, 2017), 155–156.

CHAPTER NINE

1. Lyn Mikel Brown, & Carol Gilligan, *Meeting at the Crossroads: Women's Psychology and Girls' Development* (New York, NY: Ballantine Books, 1992), 22.
2. Brown & Gilligan, *Meeting at the Crossroads*, 3.

CHAPTER TEN

1. Robert Burns, "Auld Lang Syne," version sent to George Thomson, September 1793, public domain.
2. C. S. Lewis, *The Four Loves* (1960; reis., New York, NY: HarperOne, 2017), 100.
3. Lewis, 74.
4. *It's a Wonderful Life*, directed by Frank Capra, (Liberty Films (II), 1946).
5. Capra, 01:52:03–01:52:07.
6. Capra, 02:01:46.
7. Capra, 00:26:16.
8. Capra, 02:08:49.
9. Capra, 02:08:49.
10. *The Princess Bride*, directed by Rob Reiner (Act III Communications, 1987), 00:37:29.
11. Capra, 02:01:46.
12. Krista Tippett, "Mary Catherine Bateson: Living as an Improvisational Art," October 1, 2015, *On Being with Krista Tippett*, produced by Matt Martinez, MP3 audio, 15:38–16:11, https://onbeing.org/programs/mary-catherine-bateson-living-as-an-improvisational-art/.

AUTHOR BIO

Katherine is a trauma-informed coach, currently pursuing her master's in counseling psychology with a concentration in trauma and abuse. She works with people healing from relational harm and aids them in rebuilding their connection to themselves and authentic community. Having been through community loss at several critical points in her life, she writes about what can be discovered in these liminal spaces. She is passionate about healing through deconstructing our biased sense of meaning and is a content creator and speaker on the subjects of friend breakups and our family of origin. Kat lives with her partner and four children in Denver, Colorado, where the view of the mountains makes her wish they went hiking more often. You can find her online at katherinesleadd.com or @katesleadd on "the gram."

Made in the USA
Las Vegas, NV
12 December 2024

13956339R00150